D1139165

ANOTHER CLOSE SHAVE

William Newby was born at Kingsdale Head in the Yorkshire Dales and brought up by his grandparents at Yarlsber, Ingleton. He worked with his father on a fell farm at Higher Salter near Bentham, North Yorkshire and also for a year on a big sheep farm at Whitendale. He owned two businesses before buying Edgebank Farm, above Kendal in Cumbria. William then moved south with his wife and family and bought Langworthy Burrough Farm in South Hams, near Kingsbridge in Devon. William retired and moved back to Windermere, Cumbria where he and Edna live today.

ANOTHER CLOSE SHAVE

by

William Newby

Magna Large Print Books
Long Preston, North Yorkshire,
BD23 4ND, England.

British Library Cataloguing in Publication Data.

Newby, William
    Another close shave.

    A catalogue record of this book is
    available from the British Library

    ISBN   978-0-7505-3818-3

First published in Great Britain by 2QT Limited (Publishing)

Copyright © William Newby 2012

Cover illustration © mirrorpix

Published in Large Print 2013 by arrangement with 2QT Limited

Magna Large Print is an imprint of Library Magna Books Ltd.

Printed and bound in Great Britain by
T.J. (International) Ltd., Cornwall, PL28 8RW

To my wife Edna

For her help and encouragement

ACKNOWLEDGEMENTS

My daughter Annette and grandson Alexander for moving the project forward.

CONTENTS

1 Kingsdale Head   11
2 My Time at Yarlsber   15
3 Tales from Yarlsber   18
4 Grandfather and the
    Steam Engine   24
5 Helping Out at Yarlsber   27
6 Leyland Farm   30
7 Selling Two Horses   38
8 Pigs   42
9 The Blacksmith   47
10 Harvest Time   51
11 Delivering Young Pigs   56
12 Old Remedies   60
13 Jinny the Donkey   63
14 Churchwarden at Lowgill   70
15 Message to Craggs   72
16 Taking Horses to the Station   78
17 Snigging Wood   82
18 Dangers on a Farm   84
19 Cowan Bridge   88
20 Another Unwilling Horse   93

21 Circus Horse   96
22 Kicker: Another Difficult Horse   99
23 Ginger   105
24 1941: Another Spoiled Horse   114
25 Farm Sale at Yarlsber   117
26 High Scathwaite   123
27 Higher Salter   129
28 Wartime at Higher Salter   136
29 The American Army   143
30 A Story from the Past   151
31 Learning to Work a Sheepdog   156
32 Spy: Another Sheepdog   160
33 Trim: A Dog Worth a Mention   166
34 1947: The Snowstorm, Nell and
    Maddie   169
35 Another Close Shave   173
36 One-Eye Refuses   174
37 Leaving Home   179
38 Whitendale   181
39 Getting Ready to Leave
    Higher Salter   186
40 Layhead   193
41 Clifton Hall Farms   196
42 Edgebank Farm   207
43 The Salesman   216

1

KINGSDALE HEAD

I was born in the middle of a snowstorm on my father's birthday. The farmhouse was at the end of the valley, about seven miles from the nearest village. My mother had grown tired of awaiting the birth. She had organised everything for my arrival and already the midwife had occupied the spare bedroom for three days.

Now, with a pale sun shining intermittently through the clouds, my mother asked Father to harness the horse into the trap as she needed to stock up on her food supplies.

'A bad day to be setting off that distance, there'll be storms before long,' he said.

Undeterred, Mother set off for the village, with perfect trust in herself and Jock the horse. The snow came, as predicted, but she was well-wrapped up and Jock knew the road. On their homeward journey they made good progress, in spite of the combination of driving snow and the onset of dusk.

Suddenly Jock slowed and shied. Bessie called out, 'Who's there?'

A faint voice answered and she stopped the trap and peered down towards the ditch on her right.

'Who is it?' she called. 'Are you in trouble?'

'Is that Bessie from Kingsdale Head? It's Joe. I'm trapped in the ditch. Help me or I'll freeze to death.'

Bessie looked round for something to use. The rope that was always kept in the trap looked long enough. Clumsily she climbed down and attached it to the step so that it dangled down far enough for Joe to grip it. Then, climbing back onto her seat, she urged Jock slowly forward pulling Joe up the steep bank onto the road. With a struggle, she managed to help him into the trap and so took him home with her.

It was that night of heavy snow that I was born. The snow trapped the midwife there for another week, although Joe was able to get home to his nearby farm the next day.

Before he went, he told them how he came to be trapped in the ditch. 'I set out yesterday to look for't sheep on my side o't fell. I knew I'd be fine so long as I reached home a'fore dark. Where I went wrong was I left my bagging on a thru' stone instead o' carrying it

12

'cos it were hard enough walking without extra weight. As things worked out I'd to go further than I expected and by't time I'd come full circle I were faint with hunger. The snow closed in, cutting down the distance that I could see, and I couldn't find that thru' stone. To cap it all I missed seeing t'ditch and slipped and couldn't climb out, what with t'steep side and t'stone wall an' all. Ye'll niver know how glad I were to hear Bessie's voice. I'm right glad that horse sensed me there 'cos I'd begun to think they'd find me dead next morning. Ye saved me life and no mistake. Now I'd better be off home 'cos t'wife'll be worried sick. I'll give her't news about your little lad.'

That was the story I was to hear again and again as I was growing up. At the time I was a new baby, born into a harsh environment in a harsh world. The fact is that after such a long wait and a hard birthing my mother turned against me. This happens today but folk are more sympathetic nowadays and yet, even now, no one can expect a child to understand.

As it happens, my mother's hostility led to events which determined my upbringing and influenced my character, but during the rest of her life there was a personality clash between us.

One day Uncle Robert went to Kingsdale Head on his motorbike, to find out how things were, as Mother was pregnant again. On arriving in the yard, he was very concerned to find me outside, in an unkempt state. My father was busy taking sheep which he had dipped back to the fell and then he was going to bring in the second lot. This meant it would be at least an hour before he returned. The hazards of the sheep yards, only a short distance away from where I was crawling, were apparent.

Uncle Robert took me into the house and then went back to Yarlsber to talk with his parents. It was decided that the best thing to do would be for Grandmother to be taken, by horse and trap, to see for herself what needed to be done. Uncle Robert drove the horse and, when they returned to Yarlsber, they took me with them.

About two months later my sister Jane was born and, not long after that, my parents moved away from Kingsdale Head to take over the tenancy of a farm near Wray, called Leylands. On March 19th, 1931, my brother Nicholas was born and Father employed a young woman to help in the house. I stayed at Yarlsber and was brought up by my grandparents and my aunts. I visited my parents from time to time but never lived permanently with them until they moved to Higher Salter, when Father took over the hefted sheep flock, on November 11th, 1943, when I was coming up to sixteen years of age.

For nearly two years after leaving school I lived at High Scathwaite, with Uncle Robert, Aunty Nelly and my two cousins, Dorothy and James, and worked with Uncle Robert on the farm. I was happy there and found leaving difficult. Having to go to live with my parents was one of my worst days but, thinking back, there was so much different work ahead that this helped me to settle.

2

MY TIME AT YARLSBER

As well as my grandparents, there were three aunts and two of my uncles living at Yarlsber when I was taken there. As time went on, I started to listen to their stories of things that had happened in the past.

During the First World War, Grandfather

bought horses for the army. He went with a government official to farms to look at horses. His job was to see if the horse was sound and decide if the farmer could keep his farm going without it. He said the decision was not always easy, as more than once the official looked on as if he were interested. Grandfather would pick up the horse's hoof and let the official look at it, knowing that he hadn't a clue what to look for. Grandfather would then say, 'This one will go lame before it has done ten miles on a hard road.' Then the farmer would get to keep his horse.

When the war was over, Grandfather continued to buy and sell horses. He sold horses to the Post Office, B.R.S., brewers and farmers. A lot of horses would come to the farm unbroken and a few hadn't even been halter broken.

Uncle James and Uncle Robert had to mouth them and break them in, mostly for farm work, some for driving and the odd one for riding. The ones that were already broken in were nearly always sold shortly after they arrived on the farm.

Early in the year as many as fifteen horses would be on the farm, ploughing, carting dung, chain harrowing the meadows and snigging trees that had fallen during winter.

When hay time came around, Grandfather would even sell the horses that my uncles were using in the hay field. This happened more than once in spite of their objections. People who knew Grandfather called him, 'Ready money Nick,' because he would go to a lot of farms in the area before rent day and buy all their surplus stock. He also paid cash for the stock there and then at each farm he visited.

Many years later I was allowed to go travelling in the black trap pulled by a dark bay cob. It was then I saw him paying for the cattle and coming away without them, which I could not understand. Whilst driving back home in the trap, I asked, 'Why don't you pay for the cattle when they're brought to Yarlsber?'

'Now, me lad,' he said, 'those farmers have to pay their rents soon and if the money is in their pockets they have no need to worry. I get the animals a few shillings cheaper than they would make at auction. They are happy and I make a bit of profit.'

The cattle he bought would be driven to a meeting place a week later, depending on how good they were to handle. It was decided how many men were needed to drive them on to Yarlsber, to stay there to be fattened up for market.

Another time I asked the question about paying there and then was when a load of farm foods was being ordered and paid for. 'Why pay so soon,' I asked, 'when most people pay in a month or at the end of the year?'

His reply to my question was, 'When I see the bill I check it and, if it's correct, I pay up there and then. If ever goods are in short supply, I get them before the people who pay late. The suppliers know that they can depend on my money.'

3

TALES FROM YARLSBER

At Yarlsber, when I was young, I was told about these incidents when we sat round talking in the evening in the farmhouse.

Apparently they were once doing a lot of major repairs to the front end, rendering the walls and reslating the farmhouse. All the rubble had to be carted away, and this is one particular story that I remember about my

Uncle Robert. At the time he was a very young chap, in his early teens, and he was given the job of carting away this rubbish down onto what used to be an old railway track, which passed from Ingleborough down to the new railway. The track had been taken up years before and so it left a deep trench in which rubble, not rubbish, could be tipped so that it did not create an eyesore.

On this particular day he loaded up and off he went with this horse, which had been newly broken. He went down into a field called Good Land near the cemetery. The job was to fill the cart up and when he got down there he could tip the cart so that all the rubble came out and rolled down the embankment into the bottom of the track. As Uncle Robert backed the horse up against this track, after taking out the 'heck', for some reason this horse wouldn't stop and just ran back over the edge. They went straight down the bank and, as the cart hit the bottom, it landed straight up and the horse ended up sitting in the harness for a matter of seconds. Then it tipped right over onto its back. This left the horse and cart wrong side up with the hames, which stuck up six inches above the collar like spikes, sticking into the ground.

Now instead of Uncle Robert getting excited, and I don't think I ever saw him get excited about anything, he just stood there, lit a Woodbine, looked at the horse and cart and thought, 'What shall I do now?'

The horse was paddling away, wrong side up, not able to get up or move. As Robert was only young he thought, 'If I start messing about on my own, that horse is going to catch me with its legs. And there's no way I'm going to get it out anyway, because the hames are stuck so far into the ground that I can't move the cart.'

So he walked quietly back to Yarlsber and got Uncle James and Grandfather to go with him to help get the horse out of the predicament it had got itself into.

Uncle James and Grandfather set off at a rush, because they were anxious about the horse.

Uncle Robert said, 'Don't rush! Take it quietly! It'll still be there when we get there. It won't have gone anywhere!'

Grandfather was the one with urgency the main thing on his mind but he had to laugh at Robert saying that, especially when they got there and the horse was still the wrong side up waving its legs in the air, not as vigorously as before, but still waving them.

They quietly undid the chains from the back and the breeching straps and chains from the collar, and lifted the cart off the horse; because the cart was empty the three of them could manage this. They reared the cart up by its shafts and got it back on its wheels. Then they had to undo the collar strap to let the hames open, so that they could split them at the bottom and let the horse up. They got the horse up and then pulled out the hames and, to their amazement there wasn't a strap broken, not a chip on the shafts; in fact, there was no damage at all.

When they sorted it all out and got the horse back into harness Grandfather said, 'What we will have to do next time, before you come again, is to put two big boulders at the top, so that when you back the horse to the edge they will stop the horse backing over. I thought you would have done that in the first place.'

That incident was brought up many times, which is how I came to know about it. Uncle Robert's coolness impressed everyone, especially the way he sauntered home and then sauntered back. The number of horses that went through the hands of my grandfather and his sons, and the number of different incidents they had to deal with, led to this calm reaction!

The second incident involving Uncle Robert happened when he was given the job of carting coal from Ingleton Station. He went with two horses, one yoked in the shafts and one walking behind with traces on with two chains. The two chains would be hooked onto the shaft ends to help the other horse pull the loaded vehicle up hills.

Off he went, loaded up at the station and then set off back. Now they were both young horses, nicely broken in and they had to get as used to traffic as possible. There wasn't much traffic anyway, and they were used to work. On his way back Uncle Robert passed the Co-op, which at that time was at the bottom half of the centre of the village on the right-hand side coming from the station. What happened was the trace horse in front, hooked up ready to help when they pulled the cart up through Ingleton's steep main street and then up the steep hill to Yarlsber, saw its reflection in the window next to the Co-op. The horse panicked and whipped right round, pulling the other horse with it, which meant it went into reverse and the cart backed straight through the plate-glass window of the Co-op.

In big shifts and little ones they got all sorted out and again Robert didn't get in a panic. He had just sorted his horses out when the chap from the Co-op came out.

'You and your young horses on the road!' he shouted.

'They have to get used to it sooner or later,' Robert replied.

Robert got back to Yarlsber much later than expected, as the front horse took a long time to settle down. Grandfather said, 'Where've you been?'

Robert had to tell him the story and he thought, 'Well that's the end of that. I'll not be doing any more of that today.'

But Grandfather was a hard taskmaster and he said, 'Well! You'll not learn any younger! Get yourself back and get another load.'

Off Robert went for another load, but he was real cagey this next time. He asked someone he knew in the village to lead the first horse past the Co-op, so if it saw itself again he wouldn't have the same problem. He knew there was no backing out of any job you were given to do.

Grandfather had a new window put in at the Co-op that day.

4

GRANDFATHER AND
THE STEAM ENGINE

This is another story about a horse and a steam engine. Grandfather, and all other farmers and people who lived in the countryside, would vie with one another over the type and quality of their horses, just as we do now with cars.

This particular horse my grandfather had treated himself to was a very good type, which he used for driving in the trap and for riding. He would ride this horse to look at the animals on some land called Chamlers, which was about a mile and a half from the farmhouse down Green Lane. Then he would go on to another area of land which he owned on the other side of the main road towards Whinny Mire, to look at the stock in that field at the same time.

This event happened whilst all Grandfather's family were still at home: Grandmother, Uncle James, my father William,

Aunty Jenny, Aunty Edith, Aunty Helen and Uncle Robert. Grandfather had gone off with his horse to look at the cattle in the biggest field and then across the road to look at the stock in the other one. The horse was wearing a new saddle and bridle, and Grandfather was well-dressed and a very good rider. On his way back he thought, 'I'll not go back through the field, I'll go down the road and back up Green Lane.'

Well, he got halfway down towards the turning up Green Lane when over Skew Bridge came this bus with solid rubber tyres, driven by steam and making the same noise as the steam roller. The horse took fright because of the noise and the driver stopped the bus because he could see the horse was frantic. Grandfather was determined that the horse would go past and no way was he going to dismount and lead her. She would have to get used to motor vehicles sooner or later.

When the horse was parallel with the vehicle, she reared up, turned round on herself without moving her back legs and one of her legs broke under her. Grandfather had to take the saddle off her and let her hop into a neighbour's field on three legs. He took the bridle off, left the horse in the field and walked home carrying the saddle and bridle.

Uncle James and Father were working with the horses, either chain harrowing or other spring work, when they saw Grandfather with the saddle on his back and the bridle in his hand. When he got to the stile in the wall that led into the field where they were working, both James and my father saw him stop. They wondered what had gone wrong.

'Should we go over to him?' asked Father.

Uncle James said, 'No! We'd better stay here.'

After a little while Grandfather went over to them and said, 'You'd better take the gun and shoot that horse.'

'Why? What's happened?' James asked.

Grandfather told them what had happened and they realised the reason he had stopped at the stile. He was absolutely broken hearted, as it was such a beautiful horse. After what had happened, he never again made a favourite of another horse.

5

HELPING OUT AT YARLSBER

Each schoolday I would catch the school bus at the top of Yarlsber Brow, along with three other children. The bus was a Bedford and held about thirty passengers. This was at the year end of 1940, when I was still only twelve years of age, coming up to thirteen.

A situation arose which meant that I had to walk to school for a while. The flu bug swept through the area and most families had someone who got it. This affected us also. Uncle James, who was never ill, got it badly. Grandfather was not fit enough to work outside. Everyone had extra jobs to do.

My job was to go down the paddock and across two fields to the outbarn to feed the cattle with hay on my way to school. I had to wear overalls on top of my school clothes, wear old boots and carry my clean shoes in a bag.

In the shippons there were twenty or more cattle in stalls, and hay had been put in the

27

fodder gangway in front of each pair of cows or heifers. All I had to do was to pick up the hay in my arms and put it over the boskin for each pair. I did this job for three days, as Uncle James was off work for that length of time. On the third morning when I went to feed these cows and heifers as usual, I found that there was no hay in the fodder gangway. I had to go up onto the hay moo, which consisted of loose hay in bays in the barn.

I went into the barn, picked up a hay fork and climbed up the ladder to the top of the hay that was being used. I saw there was a heap of loose hay so there was no need to cut any with the hay knife. There I was, fork in hand, about to stick the fork into this pile of hay when a voice from under the hay further away shouted, 'Don't stick thi' fork into't hay! There's a man asleep there!'

I wonder if you can imagine how I felt at that moment. I knew I had to get on with the job. This I did, but I had to get my hay from a different place from where they had slept. I had to feed the cattle whatever happened.

'You shouldn't be sleeping in here,' I said.

The man who had shouted replied, 'We've nowhere else to sleep.'

He could see that I was a bit frightened

because he said, 'No need to be feared of us. We won't hurt ye, lad. I'll get t'hay down for ye.' This he did and I fed those cows as quickly as I could. Then he said, 'Don't tell yer boss, will yer?'

'No,' I replied. 'But you'd better not be here tomorrow morning because most likely somebody else will be coming. Not only that, someone will be coming down later to clean out the shippons.'

I took off the overalls, packed them in a bag and walked nearer to school past all the mud and water. Then I put my boots in the bag, laced up my shoes and found a hole in the wall where I left my bag, to be picked up on my way home. I cut across the railway line, passing under the overhead bucket line which carried gravel from Ingleborough down to the crusher near the railway siding, and so on to school. I wonder how the children of today would cope!

6

LEYLAND FARM

This farm had been vacant for some time when my parents became tenants around 1930. They had looked it over and decided it would be a good place to make their first go at farming on their own. The entrance to the place was a track from a minor road and it was about five miles from Wray.

Father and Grandfather arranged to meet the agent about a week later to make all the agreements as to the value of the two hundred ewes. They also checked the state of the fences and walls, as these had to be in as good order at the end of the tenancy as at the time of the takeover. They left Yarlsber Farm near Ingleton early in the day to travel the fourteen miles by horse and trap and arrive in plenty of time to meet the agent for the takeover.

Grandmother packed food that would see them through the day and a bag of mixed oats, bran and chopped hay was placed in the trap. As soon as they arrived at Leyland Farm the horse was unyoked, taken into the stable, unharnessed and given some of the food in the bucket in the manger, as the manger had not been used for some time.

It was a sunny spring day, time for them to have some of the food they had brought with them. When the first ham sandwich was half-eaten, they heard the horse acting up in the stable and went immediately to investigate, thinking she must have colic. They found her pulling on her halter and moving from side to side in her stall. Her iron shoes were making sparks on the paved floor.

Grandfather said, 'Look at the manger! Rats!' It was overrun with them.

Father got an old sack, wet it in the trough to add weight to it and threw it at the wall above the manger so that it would drop down on the rats. They went back into the wall in the blink of an eye.

It took time for the horse to settle down and they had to take care when going to the stall to loosen the rope from the ring in the manger. When she was outside, they put a rug over her as she was wet with sweat. The bucket had to be washed in the stream, filled with fresh feed from the bag and even then the horse was wary and had to be encouraged to put her nose in to eat.

Father and Grandfather sat to finish their food, all the time keeping watch on the horse. By the time they had eaten their meal she had settled down and the agent had arrived. They told him what had happened. It was agreed for someone to put poisoned food in carefully concealed places to get rid of most of the rats before my parents moved in.

A week or so later they moved in, after making the journey every second day to get the house ready for the furniture. They worked hard, with Father putting in long days to get the spring work done and Mother making the house as comfortable as possible. The hay crop was light, as the ewes and lambs had not been turned back to Goodber Fell and had grazed the pastures and meadows for too long. This would have been the easiest way to shepherd them until a new tenant could be found. Father had to spend many hours with his dog, Floss, pushing his sheep away from the green fields, hoping to get them settled on their part of the fell. The problem was that since the area of fell allocated to Leyland had not been grazed, sheep belonging to neighbouring farms were pushed there to graze.

Every morning Father would be on the fell at daybreak and again when the farm work was done at the end of each day. He would check his sheep and often found them close by the fell gate. He suspected they had been chased by dogs until one day he went earlier than usual, to find most of them with their mouths open, breathing heavily. He went immediately to a high point and saw a neighbour within two hundred yards. He followed the man and his dogs to his home, at a distance, as he did not want to confront him on the fell. As Father walked into the farmyard, the man was putting his dogs to bed. As he closed the kennel door, he was alarmed to see Father not six feet away.

A young man and an older woman came to the back door at that moment and the woman said, 'What's this visit in aid of?'

Father replied, 'I want to know why this man is trying to chase me and my sheep off the fell, when he knows I have gates for two hundred ewes on there.'

The man denied everything and the woman said, 'You've no proof.'

Father replied, 'I do have proof. I followed him down off the fell.'

The woman said, 'What bi' that? He has to come home.'

'There are sheep with wool pulled, two with bite marks and also dog paw marks and, best of all, boot marks like his on the sheep trods,' Father said. His parting shot was, 'You drove the last tenant off the fell, but if it's trouble you're looking for you've found it.' And with that he walked away.

Father went each morning, not knowing what he would find, and each time he was pleased to see his ewes grazing on their area. A week or so later he arrived to find the man waiting for him and he thought, 'I wonder what the hell he wants.'

The man stepped forward, held out his hand and said, 'I've come to apologise. From now on you'll find me a good neighbour.' They shook hands and spent some time chatting together.

In the next three years, Jane and Nicholas were born and the calves and sheep made reasonable prices at the market. My parents seemed to be getting on their feet. Then, in the year Nicholas was born, there was more rain than usual. The hay was difficult to get and was of poor quality. Father was advised to put two hundredweights of nitro chalk to the acre on one of the meadows to grow extra grass, so the cows could stay out longer in the back-end and this would eke out the hay. The grass that grew was dark green and about nine inches high when the in-calf heifers went to it. After a week passed, Father noticed that they were not grazing as usual but were eating the old grass under the walls and fences.

Within ten days most of the animals aborted. This was terrible. The vet was called to take samples from each animal as she aborted, only to find it was not contagious. He could give no explanation as to why this was happening. The worry my parents had is hard to imagine. Work went on and weeks passed, but no one could find an explanation.

One day a gypsy called with his piebald horse pulling a flat cart, to see if there was any scrap iron, sacks or sheep wool he could have. There were some sacks and some tailings of wool and, in exchange, he gave a couple of pumice stones. These were used on window ledges outside or on the steps to the outer doors. Father told him that the cows had lost their calves.

The gypsy said, 'Seeing thou's let me hev these sacks and wool wi'out bickering, I'll tell thee what tha'll hev to do. Thou'll hev ti git a donkey and put her in yon meadow. That'll stop it.'

Father listened in amazement and was very

suspicious, thinking, 'This is a lot of nonsense.'

The gypsy said again, 'Thee do that lad and thi' troubles are over. Them cows are sick o' that grass and have teken to't rubbish near't walls and fences.'

'But why? What caused it?' asked Father.

'I'll tell thee next time I come to see how tha's doing 'cos if tha' doesn't listen there's no point in telling thee,' he replied. He then said, 'So long,' and left Father standing in the yard thinking over what he had heard.

He told Mother about the gypsy's advice and they decided to go to Meg's Farm the next day, to see if Mr Danson would lend them a donkey. He lent them a donkey and the horse had to walk all the way home as Maisie wasn't shod and they had to allow her to keep up. Later in the day she was taken into the field with the rich grass, both parents wondering what she could possibly do. Each day, when Father looked at the three heifers still in calf, he prayed that no more would abort. To his surprise all three held on and calved heifer calves at the right dates.

The gypsy called in. He knew Father had got the donkey and was keen to see if his advice had worked. Before anyone could speak, he said, 'Tha'll hev to get them heifers to't bull the first time they show. That's best time to mek 'em hold.'

Before he went, Father said, 'I still have no idea what the donkey could have done to stop it so quickly.'

All the gypsy said was, 'A poisonous grass, mare's tail. It meks cows abort but don't affect donkeys, who luv it. Yon donk's cleaned it out from round't field.'

After many thanks from my grateful parents, he said, 'Thi luck's changed. I'll see thi agen. All thi heifers'll go over time when thi calve and'll milk well.'

True enough they all calved and milked better than expected, as they had had a long rest. My parents always treated gypsies well throughout their farming life and, many years later, I was to use this gypsy knowledge to help a farmer with the same problem.

7

SELLING TWO HORSES

It was spring and the farm work was in full swing. Uncle James was ploughing, getting ready for putting in the crops. There were still a few sheep to lamb and most of the cattle had been turned out to grass.

Grandfather was dressed in his market clothes. Grandmother had died the previous year, a great loss to all of us, so it was Aunty Jenny who straightened his tie and made sure he looked smart. He had already packed a bag with a few essentials, as he was going to Ireland in the hope of buying horses. I was the last to finish breakfast because my jobs outside had taken longer than usual. Fortunately it was school holidays.

Grandfather turned to me and said, 'Now, me lad. I have a job for you today, so pay attention to what I'm going to say. There are two chaps coming today at 11.30 to look at two horses, the first two in the stable down the yard. Now think on, don't go off anywhere. Hang about the yard here and when they arrive tell them I'm sorry not to be here. They'll want to see each horse yoked in the cart as well as being yoked together in the chain harrow, to see what they think of them.'

The men arrived on time and I left the job I was doing to tell them that Grandfather was sorry not to be there and I had been given the job of letting them see the horses. We walked down to the stable. They talked to each other quietly as we walked along and I tried to listen. I had an idea what they were saying.

In the stable, one man looked at the horse in the first stall and the other man went into the stall of the second horse. I could tell by their expressions and their attitudes that the horses were better than they expected. One thing I had learned from watching Grandfather was never to show what your real thoughts were, or give any praise or clue that you have any interest, when buying horses. They were a bit careless, I thought, because of my youth.

After a little time I was asked to trot each horse up and down the yard to let them see if they handled well and if there were any faults in either animal's movements. One man asked me if Nicholas had said that the horses could be harnessed to the cart or the harrows, and I told him that he had. The harness was put on one horse at a time and each horse was yoked to the cart, which was a high one with wooden wheels with iron rims. After being driven up the yard, out onto the road and up to Green Lane End and back, the cart saddle was removed from each horse and replaced with a back band and chains. The two horses were taken into the croft, where they were coupled together by fastening a rope from the bit on the near side of one horse to the hame on the other horse, and doing the same again to couple them together. Then, in double harness, they were yoked to the chain harrows and driven up and down until the men had seen all they wanted. The horses were unyoked and taken back to the stable, the harness taken off and I gave each one a scoopful of feed.

By this time I was feeling a bit worried, wondering what came next! We all walked back to the car with little being said. I was thinking all was lost.

After a few minutes one man said, 'Did Nicholas say what price the horses had to be?'

'Yes,' I replied.

'Well come on, let's be knowing. It's a poor do Nicholas leaving a lad to sell his horses.'

I told them a higher price than Grandfather had told me, still worrying, hoping I had not done wrong.

The man said, 'That's a high price. Does Nicholas think we are made of money? Those horses aren't worth all that. Will he take less?'

I said, 'I'm sorry, but Grandfather told me those horses are worth the money and he knows they will do any work they are put to.'

There was a long pause. I was terrified they would say no. To my relief the bargain was struck. One of them said, 'Nicholas is straight in his dealings and we know he'll have them back if we're not satisfied.'

Trying to do the job properly, I asked, 'What about delivery and payment?' This sounds very cheeky when I think about it now!

What the man said in reply was, 'By Jove, this is a hard young man. Nicholas is training him right!' They made out the cheques using the car roof as a desk, gave them to me and shook my hand, which made me feel good, and off they went after arranging for the collection of the horses.

It was a few days before Grandfather returned. The horses had gone to their new homes. We were having our evening meal when he asked how I had done selling the horses. I told him they were sold. Aunty Jenny, who always seemed to be laughing, and not always about things that were funny, handed over the cheques with a smile.

After a few minutes Grandfather looked across the table at me. 'Did I tell you to ask that much for them?' he asked.

'That's what I thought you said,' I replied innocently. He knew darned well what I had done, but all he said was, 'I'll have to leave you to sell all my horses in future,' which was praise indeed from him.

The year was 1940 and I was twelve years old.

8

PIGS

As a young man Grandfather was a butcher by trade, although he had grown up on a farm. All the time he farmed he kept pigs, large whites. At the time I was living there, three sows were kept to breed from and the young piglets suckled to about twelve weeks old. Some would be sold to local farmers and a few would be fattened for our own use. The best gilts were kept for breeding to replace the older ones.

The war was on and food was scarce. When a pig was killed and cut up, the meat was cured in the cellar. The flitches, shoulders, hams and cheek were placed on the blue slate shelf, which was about three feet wide, on three sides of the bigger room. The meat was carefully placed on top of a layer of salt and then covered over with more salt. Any visible bones were covered with saltpetre. When the meat was cured all the salt was brushed off and the hams, flitches and shoulders were wrapped in gauze and hung on hooks in the kitchen. The odd ham or shoulder would be sold to a relative or friend, not to make money, just to help them eke out the meagre rations allowed during those hard times.

Now when the piglets had been weaned, the sow had to be taken to the boar. This was a distance of three miles, which doesn't sound a long way until you think of the size of a sow, which could weigh over twenty-score pounds. I would be about twelve years old when this job was given to me. There were no Land Rovers and trailers then. The most difficult part was getting the sow away from the farm, and many attempts were made. Aunty Jenny and Aunty Helen helped me and we each had a light board, with a handle cut top centre, to steer the pig. They helped until they could tell that the sow had decided to co-operate and then they stood watching for a time to see what progress I was making.

The first pig I took moved slowly and I soon realised it was going to take a long time, as she wasn't used to so much exercise. At home she would have been lying on one side suckling or, if outside in the little croft, she would have been resting out of the sun. She had only walked half a mile when down she went into the dip on the grass verge. I tried getting her up by pulling her hair, pulling her tail, jumping up and down waving my arms, but all to no avail.

I was beginning to think the job was going to beat me when a chap came by and said, 'Are ye having a bit of bother lad?'

'I've to take this sow to Nut Stile, where Mr Bass keeps the boar,' I replied.

He said, 'You've a fair way to go yet, but don't get down in't dumps. I'll get this pig on its feet.'

He went to the pig, got hold of her ear, bent down and shouted into it. She got on her feet and was away. I thanked the man, but all he said was, 'Tek thy time lad. Then tha'll meck it.'

All went well as I stayed well back to let her walk at her own speed. When she had gone nearly another mile, down she went again. I sat down on a stone sticking out of the wall and let her rest for five minutes and then I used the light flat stick, which was made so it could not bruise her, to get her up. Now she walked slower than ever but I didn't care, as long as she was making some progress.

Within sight of Nut Stile she lay down again in the middle of the road. I sat down for what seemed forever and the sow just lay there contentedly. I thought, 'I'll try what that man did.' I walked up to her lifted her ear and shouted into it at the top of my voice. Up she got and off she went towards the farm. It was then I noticed a woman and her daughter standing nearby. I felt really stupid and this must have shown on my face. They both laughed and I was just going to say, 'It's all right laughing when you've no idea what a struggle I've had,' when the woman said, 'I've seen many ways of moving stock, but that beats them all!'

I arrived at the farm with the pig. Mr Brass put her in a sty, saying, 'Leave her overnight. Come back tomorrow.' This pleased me, as you can guess.

When I returned home Grandfather said, 'Where's the pig?'

'I've to go back tomorrow,' I replied.

'That's all right, because there's another in season. You can take her and bring the first one back,' I was told.

On the return journey the big sow walked slowly but never once lay down to rest. She knew the way home, so I stayed a long way behind. She turned across Skew Bridge, passing Red Lane on her right, turned left out of Green Lane and went down the hill to Yarlsber. She certainly knew her way home! Anyone who thinks pigs are stupid knows nothing about pigs.

9

THE BLACKSMITH

The year was 1939 and I was eleven years old. The blacksmith, Bob Taylor, and his man, Ted Hebblethwaite, would come from Green Smithy when ten or twelve horses were in need of shoeing. Mr Taylor would pack a little anvil, a foot rest, rasps, nails, hammers and all the things needed for the job, in the side car of his motor cycle. He would arrive at Yarlsber with Ted riding pillion.

There was always a big fire ready in the living kitchen. Grandfather was the stoker and new shoes were placed in the fire to get red hot, as many had to be altered to fit the different shaped feet. The old shoes were removed from the horse's feet, each hoof was trimmed and each shoe made ready to fit. Whilst still hot, the shoe was pressed against the hoof, burning the horn until the shoe fit level. My job was to fetch some of the red-hot shoes from the fire in the house, whilst Uncle James helped me when he had no need to hold the horse being shod. As each horse was shod, it was returned to the stable.

Come the end of the day, with the last horse nearly finished, I was sent down to the bottom stable. When I opened the door the horses in the first two stalls were down on their sides, kicking and rolling about. I knew this was bad and I ran back to tell everyone.

Uncle James, Mr Taylor and Grandfather went to find out what was wrong and they knew at once that they had colic. The horses were made to get on their feet and walk up and down the yard, whilst all the time they tried to lie down as they were in so much pain. Both were then given a 'drench' or medication. One was perhaps a little better, but the other one showed no improvement.

Mr Taylor must have seen this many times, being a blacksmith, and he told me to go back to the house to get some feathers, put them in a bucket and be as quick as I could. As I ran to house I thought, 'What can he want feathers for? Is he joking to make a fool of me?'

Asking Aunty Jenny and Aunty Helen, I was told, 'We can't give you feathers. The only ones we have are in the pillows.'

I had to get them from somewhere and what better place than the hen cabin in the orchard? I got a flat bucket from the feed store, made my way to the hen hut, hoping to find enough feathers. I picked up all there were on the floor and in the nest boxes but these only covered the bottom of the bucket. Now in the hut there were about six to eight cockerels being fattened for the table. I caught one cockerel and plucked feathers from around its legs and did the same with five more. With each handful of feathers I took they squawked and squawked, but the noise didn't stop me and eventually the bucket was full. I ran back to Mr Taylor still hoping it wasn't a joke.

'Where did you get those feathers?' asked Uncle James.

'I'll tell you later,' I replied.

Mr Taylor took the bucket of feathers from me and lit them with a match, which made them smoke with no flames. He held the bucket under the nose of the badly affected horse and said, 'If this does no good there's no hope.'

The horse was forced to breathe the smoke into its lungs and in a short time he started to improve. As time went on he was back to normal, but Uncle James stayed with him to make sure.

By this time it was 9.30 p.m. and a big meal was ready in the house. Everyone sat round the table enjoying the meal and chatting about the horses and all that had happened that day.

'Where did you get all those feathers William?' asked Aunty Helen.

'I got them from the hen hut in the orchard,' I replied.

'There wouldn't be enough feathers in there,' she said, 'because the hut was cleaned out yesterday. So where did you get them?'

'I'd to get some from each cockerel,' I said.

They couldn't stop laughing. Grandfather was a man not given to laughter and a smile was the best you would see, but he couldn't help joining in with the rest.

Next morning both aunts went down to the hut to see what damage I had done. What they found were six cockerels looking as though they were not wearing trousers, as I had plucked all the feathers from round their legs.

I was in the house when they returned, finishing my breakfast. They both tried to look angry but they could hardly tell Uncle James, who was there, what they had found for laughing.

10

HARVEST TIME

At Yarlsber, Cemetery Meadow had stooks of oats, an outstanding crop that had been cut with the binder pulled by three shire horses. Even as a young lad I knew that, as there were so many stooks close together all over the field. Around the field, a path had been cut with scythes by hand wide enough for the horse-drawn binder to get round the field without treading on any part of the standing crop. Each scythe had a frame fixed to the bottom of the pole to direct the straw into a swathe, to be picked carefully by hand and then bound with straw to make sheaves.

I enjoyed the harvest as we all worked together. Aunt Helen taught me how to make the band of straw to tie round each sheaf and then the sheaves had to be picked up, one in each hand, to stack together in eights. These were called stooks. For the time being these sheaves stood against the wall, out of the way. Uncle James and Uncle Robert cut the corn with long-handled scythes with such ease because the scythe blades were razor sharp, and the three of us could not keep up.

Each day my two aunts and I had to go to the corn field to put right any stooks that had fallen over, until the time came and the weather was good enough to pull the stooks apart and put the butt ends of the sheaves to the wind to dry, ready to be carted home to Yarlsber to be made into round stacks in the croft, not far from the buildings. Uncle James and Grandfather spent many hours thatching the four round stacks and one oblong stack in the croft. They were now on hard ground ready for when the threshing machine came.

Sunday was the day when relations and friends called. They were very interested in everything on the farm as some of them were from town and to them this was like a holiday. When they were taken to see the stacks of corn that were so well made and so large, each with a thatched roof, they wanted to know how it was possible to make them so perfect out of sheaves that had been handled so often.

Later in the year the threshing machine came, pulled by a traction engine with iron wheels with thick rubber on the rims and a big flywheel in its right side. When, at last, it was all set level and the long belt that drove the thresher was the right tension, two men climbed on top of the thresher to cut the band around each sheaf and feed it down the chute into the mechanism that took out the grain that was bagged off at the side. The straw came out at the back into another chute called a bottler that made big bundles, tied with strong string, which were stacked in the barn for cattle fodder. Neighbours came to help and, when the thresher moved to their farms, Uncle James helped them in return.

My aunts brought out a wicker basket with lots of food and a large can full of tea, so there would be no need to stop threshing until it was time for the midday meal.

Two men with forks tossed the sheaves to the two men on the thresher and two men were in charge of the grain bags, to make sure they were not filled too full, making them too heavy to carry.

My friend Dennis Morphet and I had the easy job, or so we were told at the time, and this was to change the bags when they were full of chaff and carry them round the corner into a loosebox. We had to make sure one of us was always there to change the lever to the empty bag before the other bag was too full. If that happened the thresher would clog up.

We took turns. I would take a bag and then Dennis would take the next, and by the end of the morning we were shattered. The dust and sharp particles were making breathing difficult, our eyes were red and swollen and sweat had made the dust stick to every part of our bodies.

The time came for the midday meal and Dennis and I followed Grandfather into the house. Poor Grandfather was in trouble. I had never heard anyone tell him off before. Why had we been chaffing without masks or goggles and why for so long, as we were only young boys? What would Dennis's mother have to say when he got home? I felt sorry for Grandfather and said we were alright, but no one listened. Before we could have our meal, we had a bath, put on clean clothes and had the white of an egg trickled into each eye, as they were so red and itched so much that it was difficult not to rub them and make them worse.

When the meal was over, with nobody saying a word, Dennis and I left the table. I whispered to Grandfather that I was going to walk some of the way with Dennis back to his house. He nodded and we were gone.

I walked with Dennis to Green Lane, finding breathing very difficult as the dust had got into my lungs.

Mr Morphet's van stopped near us, as he was on his way to pick Dennis up. I got into the van with Dennis's help and Mr Morphet went on to Yarlsber. He told us to stay in the van as he was going to take me to see Dr Marks in Ingleton, because my breathing sounded as if I was whistling, but first he went to tell everyone. Aunty Jenny came along to the doctor's surgery, all the time apologising for causing so much inconvenience. Dr Marks examined both of us. The dust had not affected Dennis's lungs and only his eyes were affected.

I spent a week in bed and the doctor called most days. He advised them not to let me go into any building where there could be any dust and, even when I had recovered, I must wear a mask. Even to this day, I wear a mask when I am doing any dusty jobs!

11

DELIVERING YOUNG PIGS

It was a weekend in spring 1941 and, as always, Grandfather had a job for me.

'I want you to take six, three-month old, pigs to Mr Chapman's. It's a farm with the entrance on the opposite side of the road to Hill Inn up in Chapel-le-Dale. Your Aunty Helen will go with you.'

'How am I going to do that?' I asked him.

'With a horse yoked in the black cart,' he replied.

My thoughts, at that time were, 'I hope this is going to be a chance to drive one of those new horses that came three weeks ago.'

I had taken a fancy to one particular horse, which was the best driving horse I had ever seen. In a stall, further along in the stable than his stall, there was a ginger horse, which had been taken in part-exchange for a young horse. When seeing her for the first time, as she came down from the lorry, I couldn't believe that Grandfather would buy such a thin horse. She had long unkempt hair, a 'ewe' neck and deep hollows over her eyes. She must have wondered why her life had changed so much when feeding time came and every feed was of the best. She had to wear a rug to help her cast her long dead hair and she even wore the rug when she was taken outside into the croft for exercise.

Ginger was the horse Grandfather began to get ready for the trip. As he removed her rig, ready to put on the harness, knowing I was displeased he said, 'You'll have to take this horse because she won't mind the pigs in the trap. That other horse wouldn't be safe. This horse will.'

I led her to be yoked in the black trap, which Grandfather had made for his butcher's business in Manchester many years before. It was well made, with an area behind the passenger seat where a rope net had been placed ready to hold the six pigs. The pigs were loaded and made secure and off we went.

'Why do you look so glum?' Aunty Helen asked. 'Cheer up.'

'Just look at that horse,' I replied. 'I do not feel proud driving a horse that looks like her.'

'Don't be silly,' she said, 'this horse's only

fault is that she's getting old. You'll be old one day.'

Mr Chapman's farm was about five miles from Yarlsber. My memory of this farm is that it was through a gateway opposite Hill Inn as Grandfather had said, and along a track that seemed to go on for ever. Even when you got close to the place it couldn't be seen, as the house and buildings were hidden behind rocks. The way to the front door was between two massive rocks. It was a place that made a great impression on me, as did the people living there.

We unloaded the pigs into a clean loose-box and the men were very pleased with them. 'Put that nosebag on that horse and tie it to that ring near the door,' said one of them. 'We'll go and have summat to eat. It's all ready.'

Inside the house, with hands washed, we all sat around the table. On the floor near the fire was a hand-pegged rug, but other-wise the floor was blue slate. The table had a white scrub top and everything was spotless. The only chair was a rocking chair.

We had a cracking meal and then the lady paid Aunty Helen cash for the pigs. I enjoyed every minute. Outside, after thanking her for the meal, we had to look at some of the livestock. This took more than an hour and proved very interesting. Aunty Helen finally said we must go, but we had a struggle to get away because they loved having visitors.

As we set off along the track, Ginger knew she was going home. Her head was up, her ears were forward and she had a spring in her step. Soon we had closed the last gate and were back on the tarmac road. Ginger set off.

Aunty Helen said, 'Slow that horse down. She's going far too fast. You'll have her falling.'

She sounded so annoyed that I pulled at the reins as hard as I could to make Ginger take it easy, but no, Ginger was having none of that.

Now Aunty Helen said, 'You'll have to let her have her head.'

This I did and it worked. Ginger knew what she was capable of, better than me. We arrived back home in much less time than I had thought possible. Grandfather came to help unyoke Ginger and asked, 'How did this horse do then? You were so sullen about taking her this morning.'

I smiled and said, 'Ginger gave me a surprise.'

Later Aunty Helen said, 'William got a

shock. He couldn't believe how much stamina and speed she was capable of.'

Ginger was groomed, fed, given a little water and bedded down. She was to be checked again after the evening meal. When we were all sitting around the table, Aunty Helen told them every detail of our time at the farm and our homeward journey. When she had finished, Grandfather turned to me and said, 'When you left this morning, you had no idea what that horse was capable of. When looking at any horse, even one you don't think much of, remember that it may be different from what you expect. That's another good lesson for you.'

And so my farming education continued.

12

OLD REMEDIES

During the winter of 1940 and the spring of 1941, all the horses in the bottom stable got strangles. This is like mumps in humans. Under the top jaw and the bend of the neck there is swelling, and the horse can't eat and has great difficulty in drinking. The stable held six horses in stalls and had a foaling area at the far end. The vet had to come, which was very rare then as most farmers had cures of their own and money was scarce.

The vet examined the horses to confirm what Grandfather already knew. He then gave each horse a round ball of oatmeal covered in stuff smelling of liquorice, a smell I would know today as I got the job of looking after these horses. The vet had me helping him and he showed me how I had to hold the horse's tongue outside the mouth with one hand and, with the other hand, put this ball of medication behind the lump way down the horse's mouth so that the horse had no option but to swallow it. Another remedy which had to be used along with this was hay tea. This, as it sounds, is good hay put into a bucket and boiling water poured onto it, filling the bucket. This was a big job for me so Uncle James helped me sometimes, as he was on the mend from flu. When this hay tea was brewed and cool enough to drink, each horse had to have its fill, which meant there had to be a backlog of tea to cope. The set boiler in the wash house was on most of the time. Grandfather kept it going and I was the 'fetch and carry' boy.

Each day was better than the previous one. The horses began to trust me and soon all but one would willingly let me get hold of its tongue and put the ball of medication down its throat, as if knowing it would give relief. The horse that gave me the most trouble was, as you would guess, a seventeen-hands, black gelding. He was quiet to handle, but no way was he going to let me get hold of his tongue. All he did was hold his head out of my reach. I gave some thought to this and my idea was to get hold of a rope halter and put this over his night halter; then, climbing into the manager, I could tie him as near as possible to the metal hay rack that was bolted through the wall. Carefully and continually talking to him, whilst terrified for fear he would panic, pull back and hurt himself, I managed to get to him to take the black medication. First I let him smell at it and when he licked it he found it was a taste he liked. After that he would take the medication from my hand.

All the horses improved slowly with the care they were given. The hay tea played a big part in their recovery, along with lots of straw bedding and the heavy rugs they had over them. In time, after warm bran mashes, chopped hay and exercise, all but one got back to work. The horse that didn't was a gelding, a dark bay, with no white on him anywhere.

The spring came and the horses were turned into the lush grass fields, with some showing loss of flesh after their ordeal. The field work was put off as long as possible to let the horses get back to normal. The vet came to examine the dark bay gelding and found he had a bad heart. We were all depressed when the lorry came for him, as he was the best worker before he got the strangles.

13

JINNY THE DONKEY

In 1941 my parents farmed at Craggs Farm, Tatham, near Bentham. My sister, Jane, and brother, Nicholas, were always up to mischief. Nicholas was ten and Jane was eleven at the time.

Now Father bought a donkey, about twelve hands and a very good type. She had been well broken to ride and also to harness by Mr Danson from Wennington, and her name was Jinny. Father, when he bought her, also bought the harness which fitted her, because donkeys have bigger heads than horses and she needed a special neck collar, which split open at the top and fastened together with a strap and buckle. This collar, when open at the top, would be put on from under the neck and then fastened together before the hames and the rest of the harness.

The evenings were getting lighter and, when Father finished his day's work, he made a very good strong cart, the right size for Jinny, using some shafts and wheels with rubber tyres which he had collected for the job. He yoked Jinny in the shafts and called Jane and Nicholas outside. They couldn't believe their eyes, as they had had no interest in what was going on in the barn. They were delighted when they realised that all this was for them.

There were six or eight, twelve-by-eight Pilkington hen cabins on the farm, full of hens. Some were in the front pasture, some in Bradshaw Meadow and one in the pasture past the water trough. There were three breeds of hens: white leghorns, exchequer leghorns and Sussex. When Nicholas and Jane had driven Jinny down the track to the meadow gate, turned around and got back to where Father and Mother were standing, Nicholas wanted to carry on driving.

'Can we clean out a hen cabin?' he asked.

'Yes,' Father replied. 'Take a shovel and brush, clean out the cabin into the cart and empty the contents on the grass. Then go to the barn for some chopped straw for the nest boxes.'

Off they went, making as many backward and forward journeys as possible. When they had finished, they wanted to feed the hens in the cabin at the far end of Bradshaw Meadow, as they were enjoying riding in the cart. Meantime Jinny's mood had changed and Nicholas could not make her trot as usual; at the best, a slow walk was all he could manage. When the hens were fed, the eggs put into a basket with chopped straw in to prevent them cracking and they were ready to go, Jinny refused to move.

Sticks or whips were not allowed, so Nicholas said, 'I know what we can do. I'll hold the reins and you touch Jinny's rear end with the bristles of the stiff brush.'

This Jane did but, instead of just touching Jinny's back end, the brush somehow slipped between Jinny and the cart. Nicholas, holding the reins, just kept his balance. Jinny's long ears were flat against her neck, she made the strange noise donkeys make and she was going flat out for home. Every stride she took, the bristles pricked her back end. Jane managed to get back on her feet, holding onto the side of the trap and, with a struggle, retrieved the brush just in time for Nicholas to control Jinny. When she stopped they sat on the sides of the little cart, hoping Father hadn't been watching out for them.

Jinny was unyoked, put in her loosebox, her harness removed and she was brushed, fed and petted.

When the evening meal was over, Father asked, 'What made Jinny gallop across the field like she did?'

Both sat for a while, knowing the truth was the only way. They had been seen!

Jinny was kept in a paddock behind the house. If the weather was bad she could shelter in the little loosebox that had at one time been a pig sty, and also she was handy for Nicholas and Jane to spend time with. Now the two horses were in the front pasture and when the family were having afternoon tea around four thirty, with Father sitting by the window, he saw the two horses galloping to the far side of the field. He saw them turn with their heads high and they were snorting. Before he could say anything he saw Jinny coming round the corner, making for them. As she got near, off they went again trying to get away from this strange animal with long ears.

Father said, 'Finish the meal and then we'll sort this out,' but all the time he was keeping an eye on them.

Once outside, Nicholas, Jane and Father went to see how Jinny had got out of the paddock. They found both gates unfastened. Nicholas looked at Jane and then they both told Father that the gates were closed and they hadn't been through them.

Back in the front field, the horses had stopped galloping away from Jinny and stood together with their necks at full stretch, sniffing at her. Father got a bucket with some oats in, together with Jinny's halter, and told Nicholas and Jane to stay where they were whilst he put Jinny back in the paddock behind the house. He told them to make sure the gates were fastened.

'Don't go near the donkey,' he said. 'The hens need feeding and I have my jobs to do. We've wasted too much time.'

After supper Father went out back to check the gates were fastened and to give Jinny a small scoop of feed. Nicholas and

Jane were moody; they thought they were in the 'dog house' and that Father didn't believe they had fastened the two gates.

As always, Father was outside early next morning. He found the two horses standing near the wall near the water trough and, when he looked again, there was Jinny standing between them, as calm as you please. He couldn't believe it, as he had made sure the gates at each side of the sheep yard had been fastened.

The milking was done by hand, the milk then cooled and run down into a twelve-gallon kit. With a horse yoked in the milk float, Father took the milk to the milk stand, about half a mile away.

At breakfast he said, 'Have either of you looked through the window this morning?'

They ran to the window and they saw Jinny not fifty yards away, looking innocent. Before they could say anything, Father said, 'Sorry I doubted you last night, but I couldn't see how Jinny could have unfastened two gates.' He explained what had happened. Each gate was fastened from the stoop to a stout nail on the gate. Jinny had played with the chain with her top lip until the chain link came off the nail. She then pushed against the gate and tried the second gate, succeeding again.

Father met Mr Danson at Bentham the following Wednesday and was asked, 'How's Jinny?'

'Very well and the kids love her,' Father replied. 'Just one thing: how much time did you spend teaching her to open gates?'

Mr Danson laughed and said, 'I had to put proper fasteners on my gates. You'll have to do the same.'

Nicholas often rode Jinny and sometimes she would be mischievous and try to buck him off. He would ride her to bring in the milk cows and go to the outbarn, two fields from home, if Father was working there. At weekends Nicholas and Jane wanted to do everything properly, with Jinny harnessed in her little cart.

They couldn't wait for the hay to be in rows after Father made little shelvings for the cart. When the first hay was ready, Jinny's cart was loaded with three rounds, a rope was put over the hay to hold it on and it was taken to the barn. Each load was better than the previous one, as Nicholas wanted his load to look like the loads that were put on the full-sized cart Father and his man brought to the barn. The last load of the day for Jinny was by far the best, as it had four rounds made tidy and square to look just right. As Nicholas and Jane arrived at the barn, Father's load had been taken off. Jinny turned to back her load up the steep rise into the barn and, as before, she put her ears flat back on her neck to push with all her strength. Seeing her do this made Father and the man laugh and they came to give a push.

To finish this story, I saw Jinny each time I went to Craggs. I never lived there because I lived with my grandparents, but to this day I think she was the best donkey that was ever put in harness.

14

CHURCH WARDEN AT LOWGILL

During the time Father farmed Craggs Farm the family attended Lowgill Church, where he was churchwarden. It was Easter Sunday evening when they got home from church to find all the new calves and young stock that had not been turned out as yet, plus two horses from the stable which were on hard keep because of the spring work ahead, outside in the front meadow. All the shippon, barn and stable doors were wide open. The wheelbarrow was upturned in the midden and lots of other things were knocked over or thrown about the farmyard.

The first thing Father and Mother worried about was if whoever had done this had ransacked the house. Instead of walking, they ran the rest of the way to find thankfully that nothing had been done to the house. Everyone changed into their working clothes and began getting the animals back inside. The horses were difficult to catch because they had got wound up from watching the calves galloping around. Getting the young stock was very difficult, as they had no idea what to do when they were gathered together. All they wanted was freedom.

The family was shattered by this time and Father was calming down from the anger he felt at first. The stupid thing was that there were only four young men in the area and this meant that their names soon came to mind. Father and Mother talked it over and decided not to do anything about it. However, when Father was next at the cattle market he would remark to the ones he suspected that they must be good at opening gates and doors. One thing for sure, they would know what was meant by his remark.

None of the animals suffered any after-effects from their few hours of freedom, even though most of them were wet with sweat after galloping about. It was some time before all the tools and the barrow were cleaned and back in place, especially those buried in the midden. It was not long before Father gave up his job as churchwarden and only went to church every now and then, as he didn't want to leave the farm unattended.

15

MESSAGE TO CRAGGS

One day in 1941, Grandfather sent me to Craggs Farm with a message for Father. I don't remember the message but I do remember that I met a really good-looking horse. The horse I rode for this journey was black with two white socks, a white blaze and was fourteen hands. This was a horse that was used for driving or riding.

When I arrived, my Mother greeted me by saying, 'For once you've got here when you can help Dad. He's in the barn with a horse that's in harness and won't move, even though he's tried to 'tice it with oats in a bucket. He's tried petting it and now he's just sitting in the trap, in the hope she'll get tired of waiting and set off on her own.'

The reason Father had yoked this horse inside the barn was because he was doing it all by himself; having her in the barn with the doors closed meant she couldn't get away from him. He hoped that as soon as the horse was safely in the trap Mother could open the barn doors, get quickly out of the way and let the horse come out into the front field. But, with the doors wide open, nothing happened.

I rode my pony into the yard near the barn and both the horse and Dad looked surprised. I could see this very good-looking horse, standing as if she had no intention of moving. I carefully rode my horse closer and closer, because I didn't want to panic either of the horses. When my horse was about a stride away from the other one, I backed her away; this made the horse in harness stretch her neck to smell at my black horse. Very carefully, the piebald horse followed my horse into an uneven field of about five acres.

After going up and down this field a couple

of times, letting them walk slowly, I sent the black on a bit faster until both were trotting at an easy pace. The horses were then unharnessed and groomed in the stable and fed and watered before we went in for a meal. I rode back to Yarlsber before dark.

Now that piebald horse was very good looking, with striking colouring. She was fifteen hands, with little or no feather, and everyone turned to look at her whilst taking very little notice of other horses. A week after she had been driven in harness, there was a farm sale at Catlow, a farm over Lythe Fell, six or seven miles from Craggs on the way to Slaidburn. The entrance to Catlow Farm was about a mile further on towards Slaidburn than the farm buildings.

My father decided to use the piebald horse and take a short cut along an old sheep track. Mother had gone along for the ride and for the change of company. Unknown to my father, the river had been in flood earlier in the winter and this had made its bed much lower. When they got to the river they could see what had happened, as the banks were steeper and the water deeper.

Mother had harsh words to say, as she couldn't hope that this newly-broken horse would even attempt to cross. The horse looked at the river for a few minutes and then carefully went down the bank into the water and out across to the other side. She carried on up a very steep hill to the farm.

All the people who saw the horse coming in the distance and crossing the river, in harness, couldn't believe it. It was well known how the previous owner had failed with her; this man was at the sale and watching with everyone else. He couldn't believe his eyes, as he had done everything he knew to get her to work in harness, even down to using the big whip. My father knew she had been ill-treated from the way she behaved. The man was a gypsy, although he lived in a house, not a caravan, and he did a lot of horse trading. He had sold her to Father knowing her fault, after giving up hope of ever getting her to drive in a trap or flat cart. When he saw this really good-looking and colourful horse only ten days later, he was amazed and immediately wanted her back. Father was brilliant with horses and, of course, he wasn't willing to sell.

A little later in the year, the gypsy caravans and horses were parked on some open land about two miles from Craggs. When anything like this happens, the news travels quickly. Now the piebald horse was being kept in the 'bull coppy' at Craggs, a field that ran close to the road. At breakfast Mother said, 'That horse needs to be put out of sight or it will be missing one of these nights.'

That night the horse was put in a loosebox and the door was locked and bolted. Strange as it may seem, around two o'clock in the morning the dogs barked and wouldn't stop. Father got dressed and went outside, keeping to the darkest places. He could see three chaps from where he stood, so all he could do was encourage the dogs to bark even more. This made the men uneasy and they went away. Father waited for a while, then returned to the house and lit the lamp to let them know that they had been heard. He still had the horse, because of Mother's foresight.

The piebald horse was one of the best-tempered, likeable horses that Father ever owned and one he hoped to keep. Wherever he took her, people would come over to pet her and say complimentary things to her. The problem was that the man from whom Father bought the horse wouldn't stop pestering him, making bigger and bigger offers. Finally it was decided with Mother back at Craggs that it might be best to sell her back to him. In the country, it was thought that no good would come from an animal someone coveted. This decision was not taken lightly because of the way she had been treated in the past.

The deal was done and the man and his brother came to collect the horse. They came in a flat cart and they took their horse out of the shafts, intending to replace it with the piebald. Father, Mother and Nicholas were looking on. As soon as the piebald heard the man's voice, she changed from her quiet usual self to being flighty and nervous, which upset both Father and Mother. The money was offered back but refused. The men couldn't harness her into the cart, so they tied her to the back.

Father watched her go with a heavy heart and although he enquired about this very special horse many times, he never got an answer. The point here is that horses are clever and do understand who they can trust.

16

TAKING HORSES TO THE STATION

It was spring 1941 and the Easter holidays from school. My job for the day was to take two horses to Bentham Station. This meant taking three horses, one to ride, with the other two coupled together at the right-handed side of the horse that I was riding. To help control them, my horse wore a neck collar and a rope from the horse nearest to her, which was passed through a ring halfway down that side, which I held. This gave me the leverage I would need, if they tried to pull away.

I was given strict orders not to let them trot, just let them walk. There was no way I would try to go faster than a walk, as one of them was not fully broken and everything was a new experience for him.

'We'll follow you in the car and be at the station in time to help load these two onto the train, then you can take Daisy to Green Smithy to be shod,' said Grandfather.

When three horses travel side by side, they need more than half of the road. Thankfully I only met two cars and they pulled into gateways and stopped their engines to let me pass. One driver said, 'Tha's got thi' hands full, lyle feller. How far is't goin?'

'Bentham Station,' I replied.

'Tha'll hev to keep thi' eye on that young un when tha' gets theer,' he said.

As I turned down Station Road in Bentham, Uncle Rob's car came up behind and followed, at a safe distance, down the long entrance to where a horsebox had been backed into a siding. An engine was still being used as the three horses walked down past the entrance.

Uncle Rob stopped the car and Grandfather got out and closed the gate because he could see the young horse acting up. The porter had the door down, with the partitions slanting towards the doorway, ready for the first horse. I held Daisy well back. The porter took hold of the black horse, led him into the far stall and tied him there. He then put the partition across. When the young gelding's turn came, as soon as his front feet came in contact with the wooden ramp, he reared up and squealed, pulling back and taking Grandfather and Uncle Rob with him. I wondered how it would be possible to get him inside the horsebox when he wouldn't go anywhere near. I watched Grandfather take off his jacket and then his waistcoat and wondered what he would do next. The waistcoat was placed over the gelding's eyes and tucked inside the halter, to hold it in position.

The porter said to me, 'Go into the office and bring the enamel jug full of water standing near the tap and be quick about it.'

I thought he was pulling my leg but dared not object. I returned with the jug of water, still wondering. The porter and Uncle Rob held the gelding, still struggling, whilst Grandfather held first one ear and poured water in and then did the same with the other ear. He gave the lead rein to me, saying, 'Walk him up to the gate once or twice.'

This I did and after a short while the porter took the rein from me, when the horse was nearing the horsebox. To my surprise he walked in without hesitation.

Hay was put in the racks and feed in the cast iron trough inside the compartment, where the groom travelled, if one was needed. It was from here that water, hay and feed were put through for the long journey.

My next job was to take Daisy to Green

Smithy to be shod. Mr Taylor wanted know all the details about the other two horses. After listening to my story he said, 'Why did you bring Daisy? I would have thought you had enough on your plate taking two horses.'

'Neither horse had been ridden,' I replied. 'Grandfather told me that Daisy would control the young gelding.' And she did.

Mr Taylor laughed, as did his son Dennis, and said, 'Old Nicholas never misses a trick, getting two jobs done for the cost of one.'

When Daisy had her new shoes on, her hooves oiled and mordax studs in place to stop her slipping on the tarmac, I let her walk all the five and a half miles back home. This only took forty-five minutes, because this big seventeen-hands horse enjoyed herself when she was homeward bound.

17

SNIGGING WOOD

Grandfather was a man who couldn't see you doing nothing and one thing he hadn't time for was playing and wasting time. So to keep me busy, he'd give me any job there was. This particular day, my brother Nick had come over to stay at Yarlsber. He wouldn't have been so old, perhaps nine years.

A new horse had come and Grandfather said, 'Well, I've a job for you. Take her and put the neck collar, head collar and chains on her and get yourselves down the cow pasture. There are two trees there with the branches cut off, ready to be moved. Snig them home but bring them one at a time, meaning the trunks, and leave the thinner lengths till last.'

The chains from the neck collar go back to a wooden sway, which keeps them apart; the snigging chain is hooked to the centre of this sway and then fastened round the logs to bring them home. Well, we got all hooked up and went across the stream, with the horse behaving well. Then we ran into a problem because there was no track up the steep field and we had to move slantways. By doing this, the log rolled, taking the horse with it down the bank. The reason for this was that the chains on the horse were too low and were rubbing on her hind legs. It was a good thing that the horse had been well broken, as most horses would have started kicking. Instead this horse kept level with the log and they both finished up back by the stream.

I now had to find a way round the problem, because I wasn't going to be beaten. Luckily I had a piece of rope long enough to go from one chain to the other over the horse's rump, which I hoped would keep the chains well away from her back legs. I turned her round, coupled up to the other end of the log and led the horse back to start again up the hill.

This time, although the log kept rolling, the horse was able to keep going because my plan worked and the rope kept the chains off her legs. When we got the heavy trunk back to the yard, my Grandfather looked at the set-up and said, 'Oh. That's how you've done it. I was wondering where you were. Good lad. For once you used a bit of initiative.'

This was praise indeed, as it was not often

he gave praise. I would be twelve years old at the time. After uncoupling it Grandfather said, 'Off you go and get the next trunk and check the rope stays tight enough over her loins.'

We snigged wood all afternoon and the horse was clever enough to learn quickly the best way to get up the hill. Nick held the horse, when needed, and he still remembers doing this.

This is another example of how Grandfather trained me. He gave me jobs to do and he expected me to deal with any problems that I encountered.

18

DANGERS ON A FARM

There are always dangers to man and beast on a farm.

When my father was a young man he was given the job, with a young horse again, of carting sand from a sandpit in the field called Good Land, which is part of Yarlsber. Fortunately Uncle Robert, who was only a young lad at the time, went with him. My father wouldn't have been so old. They were still altering and repairing the front end of the house and he had gone down with a horse and cart and backed up to the sand quarry. He was more or less loaded up, digging from the face of the sand which was approximately six-feet deep.

Uncle Robert was watching when, all of a sudden, the face collapsed and buried my father. He was in an upright position but the sand still covered his head. Robert, even as a young boy, was calm and quick-witted and he scratched with his hands to find my father's head. He got to him and shifted the sand from around his head and neck, so that he could breathe.

Now Robert got in a panic and ran to Yarlsber to get Grandfather, Uncle James and my aunts to help to get Father out. The horse stood quietly, which was a good thing as no one was watching him. They got my father out, put him on top of the sand in the cart and took him home. He was in bed, having crushed his lungs, which caused pneumonia. He took ten months to recuperate. I'm glad he made a full recovery or I wouldn't have been here to tell the story.

The next story is about a horse called Daisy. She was a grey, sixteen-hands high, with clean legs. Uncle James thought the world of her because she could get a lot of work done without any problems. One day she went missing and I, a young boy, was sent to look for her. I went round the field twice, thinking I might have missed her in a corner. It may sound strange to say you can go round a field and miss seeing a horse, but this field was uneven and it was possible not to have spotted her.

After searching again, I knew she wasn't there. All the gates were closed but fortunately I went down to the gate that led into the outbarn yard and found that it was unfastened. What the horse had done was pushed the gate open with her chest, gone through and the gate had swung to behind her. She had walked into this tiny paddock through which ran a stream. There was a barn there with a lean-to, into which Daisy had gone for shelter. In this place there was a deep concrete tank, nearly ten-feet wide, eight-feet deep and twelve-feet long, which was half full of liquid from the shippon. This tank was built into the ground and had a concrete top.

Daisy was a big horse and she must have

been stamping, as horses do if their legs are caked with mud, because when the mud dries on it causes their legs to itch. The top of the tank had cracked and given way, letting her fall in. Uncle James and I arrived at about the same time that Daisy heard us coming and, in panic and with extreme effort, she managed to get out of the tank.

Uncle James caught Daisy, who was shaking all over, and told me to get a bucket and brush from the barn. He took her to the stream to get water to clean her up and get rid of the stinking smell on her body and legs.

Before washing her, we could see there were cuts on her chest, legs and hind quarters, and some of them were quite bad. We calculated that she must have been in the tank half an hour, as earlier in the day Uncle James had been to feed the cows in the barn, and she wasn't there then. When we finished cleaning her up, we walked her home and washed her again with warm water and Lux flakes, then rubbed her down with straw and finally sawdust. Meanwhile the vet had been called to stitch the worst of the wounds.

Daisy stayed inside about two weeks being nursed and petted until she was her old self again. Uncle James went to see her every opportunity he got, because he was so fond of her. When the wounds were on the mend, she was turned into a paddock near home so that we could see her often.

It came time for her to work again and I was sent to bring her into the stable. I wondered how she would behave, as she was a very lively horse. If she was on the road or anywhere with a horse ahead, she had to pass. When I'd harnessed and yoked her in the cart, it seemed as though she was looking forward to working again. Everybody was delighted at her recovery and all the neighbours said they were pleased to see 'The Big Grey' back at work. She was one proud horse!

19

COWAN BRIDGE

I had a lot to do with horses from an early age. Whenever anyone went with the horse and trap, I hoped to go with them. I helped by fetching and carrying, and improved as I got older. By the time I was twelve years old I could handle and ride most horses that came to the farm. From that age I was considered competent enough to take on most jobs.

I would get home from school, change into working clothes, have something to eat, and then ride pillion on Uncle James's motorbike to collect any horse within six miles of Yarlsber. We always took along a lightweight saddle and bridle so I could ride the horse home.

I remember one time when the horse I had to collect was from Cowan Bridge. After visiting the family, Uncle Rob Hird, took me in his car to the lane end. With the saddle and bridle over my shoulder, I went to the farm on my own, as it was understood that the horse would be ready for me. I walked down the lane to the farm, to find only the farmer's wife at home. As soon as we met, she said 'What do you want?'

'I've come for the horse to take her back to Yarlsber,' I replied.

The look on her face and the way she shouted left me in no doubt. She wasn't going to allow me to take the horse home.

'I'll have to take her,' I said.

'The horse is in the field. You'll have to come back again and bring someone with you,' she said.

I thought, 'I'm not doing that.' When she

had gone back into the house I got some feed from the feed bin in the stable, put it in a bucket and went into the field, hoping to be away quickly. Things didn't turn out that way. The horse put her nose into the bucket, grabbed a mouthful and then ran off. I tried a few times but each time she got a mouthful and was off. I then moved the bucket nearer to the gate into the yard, in the hope of cornering her there. This worked well and I got her through the gate and in the middle of the yard, whilst I hid behind the wall near the gate. I knew she was crafty, so I kept quiet until she had her nose in the bucket once more and then, as fast as I could, I dashed to shut the gate. I was only just in time because she spotted me and immediately, from a standing start, galloped to the gate. I hoped she wouldn't try to jump it and fortunately she stopped.

Then I had to entice her into the stable. I managed this with a struggle. She was broken to harness but hadn't been ridden. I got the bridle and the saddle on her and she had a halter on with a rope attached, so I was able to unfasten the rope and use it. I led the horse into the yard, only to find that the farmer's wife had come back outside.

'That horse has never been ridden,' she

said. 'Don't be a silly boy. You shouldn't even be near her.'

'I'm not going to be beaten,' I replied. 'I'll just take her into the field to settle her down and then see how things are.'

'Very well,' she said angrily, 'but watch yourself.'

Unknown to her, I had taken two long reins from the stable as I intended to trot the horse round in a circle to let her know I was boss. First I tied up one front leg, leaving only three legs for her to use.

After about ten times round, she was breathing heavily. I got onto her back and this she did not like, so I changed the rope to the other front leg and chased her round another ten times. The effort she needed when using only three legs took the steam out of her. I tried again to ride her, but this time with her leg still tied. She lunged about on three legs until eventually she gave in. Then I dismounted, took the rope off, remounted and rode her round the field twice, talking to her and patting her neck.

On the way back to the stable to leave the ropes that I had taken without the farmer's wife's consent, I hoped she was busy in the house and I was lucky as she was.

I rode the horse back to Yarlsber, taking

about an hour as I let the horse walk all the way. When I rode her into the yard, Grandfather was waiting for me. He said, 'You've taken long enough. Where have you been? What are you doing riding? I thought you were told to walk her back. I told you that horse hadn't been ridden.'

'She was a bit awkward to begin with,' I replied and that was all I told him.

A few days later, Grandfather met the previous owner of the horse. He wanted to know how old the lad was who had been sent for the horse. 'He's twelve, coming on thirteen,' said Grandfather.

'Well,' said the man. 'He's a right devil with a horse.'

My Grandfather never gave praise but he told that tale more than once.

20

ANOTHER UNWILLING HORSE

Horses were a part of Grandfather's business. All the time I was at Yarlsber he would be out of bed before five, making sure the horses were fed and watered, ready for work. He took pride in their welfare and always had them in top condition, not knowing when someone would call needing one.

From time to time he would go to High Scathwaite, near Greenodd, to stay with Uncle Robert and Aunty Nellie. He would stay two or three weeks each time and Uncle Robert would take him in his car to farms or horse sales, hoping to find horses for his customers.

Now there came a day when an arrangement had been made for Tom Staveley to take his cattle wagon to pick up some horses from High Scathwaite. To my surprise, Aunty Jenny had planned to stay at High Scathwaite for a week, taking me with her. This meant I would get a ride in Tom's wagon. I was about nine years old at the time and this was my first chance to ride forty miles one way. We arrived and Tom turned the wagon round, ready to load the three horses.

'Come into the house, as soon as you can, because the dinner's on the table,' said Aunty Nellie.

Hands were washed in the kitchen of this house, which I was seeing for the first time. We all went through a doorway, down a step, passing a partition with coats hanging from hooks, and sat at a round table. The plates were put in front of us loaded with food: potatoes, meat, vegetables and Yorkshire pudding. This was followed by rice pudding. Aunty Nellie was a brilliant provider. We stayed at that table, chatting about different things, until the time came for loading the horse. Uncle Robert called their pet dog, a corgi, into the kitchen and wanted her kept inside until all the horses were loaded.

Two horses went up the tailgate into the lorry with no hesitation but the third horse, a dark bay shire of seventeen hands with massive feet, took two steps up the ramp and stopped. His head was near the roof of the lorry and, because of the roof's slant and the slant of the ramp, his rear end was

94

still on the ground. After many attempts to get him loaded, the big horse was once more standing on the ramp.

Now, unknown to anyone, the corgi had got out of the kitchen and made her way under the ramp, where there were metal rests holding it ten or twelve inches above the ground. All of a sudden, the big horse lunged forward into the lorry, leaving everyone wondering what had happened.

I remember everyone laughing, when they realised the reason. That corgi was a 'heeler' and she had, from the protection of the ramp, bitten the horse's hind legs. Uncle Robert wanted to know who had let her out, but nobody really cared.

I had been invited to stay but, when the time came for the lorry to leave, I went with it because everything was so new to me. I was to stay there many times in the future; they were very special people and my memories of their kindness go back to before they were married.

21

CIRCUS HORSE

Whenever I think of my time as a boy, I remember some of the risky and stupid things my friend Dennis and I thought of doing. One time, we were off school for one of the spring holidays when Dennis arrived on his bike to pass the rest of the day with me. It was Sunday, our families had attended church and the midday meal was over. All was quiet, as it was most Sundays except when we had visitors.

We spent some time in the yard, chatting and doing nothing much. Horses came into our conversation, which was nothing new as horses came and went on the farm at regular intervals. Three new horses had arrived the previous week and were now in the croft, just up the road.

Dennis said, 'Let's go and have a look at them.'

I wasn't too keen as this was against the rules when fresh horses came, because they needed time to get settled in their new surroundings and some were unbroken. When we arrived in the small field, the three horses were standing close together, each with one hind leg resting. We sat near the wall; the sun was warm, and I was happy to sit there watching them. Two of the horses were Clydesdales, about sixteen hands each, and the third was fifteen-and-a-half hands, dappled grey with blond mane and tail and with black legs and feet. She was a picture, and she was different from any horse I had ever seen.

The three horses moved into the corner of the field to stand close to the gate that led into the big pasture. I climbed over the wall into the big pasture and walked round to see how close I could get to the grey horse. Dennis walked slowly towards the horses and their attention was on him as I climbed the gate. Without any thought, my next move was onto the grey's back. She tucked her muscles together in shock at finding this thing on her back, and then galloped at full speed down the field, towards the wall.

I hung onto her mane and gripped my legs around her to stay on, but the wall was there in a flash. At that moment I was frozen in time, not knowing what would happen next.

Had she jumped that wall, there was a drop of at least twenty feet to the tarmac road. This would have badly injured both the horse and me. Fortunately she leaned back to put her four feet forward to stop herself and, by doing this, her feet dug into the ground and she finished up with her chest against the wall. Her two front legs were vertical to the wall, her two back legs were tucked under her and I slid off, none the worse.

We couldn't move her, so I ran to the stable for a halter and two ropes, hoping no one would see me. With the halter on and the ropes round her chest, we managed to pull her onto her side. When she got to her feet at last, we looked her over, taking our time and praying she wasn't injured. The luck was with us and, when the halter was taken off, she galloped back up the field to the other horses.

A few days later she was sold to a circus for a lot of money. The day she went Grand-father said, 'What are those skid marks near the bottom wall, where some sods have been replaced?'

I had to own up. I often wonder what would have happened if she had gone over the wall, with me on her back!

22

KICKER: ANOTHER DIFFICULT HORSE

The year was 1942 and I was fourteen years old. To make extra income, my father took in other people's horses as 'stags', most of them halter broken. This is about one of these horses. She was a dark bay, four years old and a very good type. Her owner was a farmer in the area, used to handling horses, and had mouthed and broken a horse each year for his own use, keeping the newly-broken one for a few seasons. Selling an older horse that was well broken supplemented his income.

Father arrived home with this filly and he gave strict instructions, 'Keep well away from her. Never get near her rear end. If you have to go into her stall, go via the hole under the manger in the next stall.'

The horse's stall was bedded down and hay was put in the rack and feed in the manger, leaving her tied to a ring outside the door until all the stable chores were done. I stood well back as Father led the horse into her stall, putting the lead through the ring on the manger, then adding the dropper and making sure it was secure. All the time he was talking to her and patting her neck. He made his exit under the manger into the next stall, saying, 'Keep well away from her back end.'

As we sat around the table that evening, we were told the horse's full history. Apparently the owner had mouthed her, driven her in long reins and then, with help, had yoked her in the cart. The horse went crazy, kicking and bucking, and then she got away from them. She galloped down the field, throwing over and smashing the cart beyond repair, and finished by galloping around the field, kicking at the harness and the two bits of shafts still attached.

When a horse came to be sorted, Father wanted a clear understanding as to what the owner wanted. In this case, the owner handed over the haltered horse and said, 'This is the first horse we have ever been afraid of. What you do is up to you. Win or lose, I'll pay you all breakages, time and feed. The only thing is, she's no use to anyone just now. If you can't make her do, the next place will be the meat factory.'

The time came for Kicker, as we nicknamed her, to be taught a few hard lessons.

'After we make sure this horse can be controlled,' Father said, 'we'll put her in the breaking cart.'

We knew what he meant, as once a horse is first between the shafts, no one has any idea what to expect. First this horse had to go through the same lessons we always used. The only difference was that this horse could 'kick a midge's eye out' and was dangerous.

I had the job of holding the long rope attached from her girth to each front fetlock, making sure to keep well away from her hind legs. Father set her off round in a circle and, picking the time when Kicker was about to make her escape, he said, 'Pull!' which I did. The rope was pulled, taking her legs from under her at the same time as she kicked out with her hind legs. This made her do a belly flop and took the wind out of her. Kicker got on her feet, snorting and showing the whites of her eyes. She was made to go round in a circle again for about five minutes, with Father just talking to her. Then came the time when Father said, 'Whoa!', making sure I would pull the rope if needed. There was no need to pull the rope because, just as she heard the first bit of the command, she came to a standstill.

We did more of the same, making Kicker go the other way round. She made one more attempt at freedom but, as soon as she felt the rope tighten, that was enough. Next, as planned, we put her in the breaking cart. All went well and then she started to kick. 'Give the rope a pull, but not too hard,' said Father. This I did, but before I had any time, she kicked again and one leg went over a shaft.

'Don't pull the rope now,' Father said, 'or we'll injure her.' To my surprise, he took no notice of the horse's leg over the shaft. Talking to the horse, he said, 'If that's how you want to play, we'll go along with you.'

She hopped along on three legs for about two hundred yards and must have realised that the only way out of the mess was to kick again which she did, just once, then she went on with no more trouble. The ropes were taken from her front legs and she was driven around the field in the cart for an hour or so.

I brought another horse in chains, and a set of chains with a back band for Kicker. They were put in double harness, yoked to the chain harrows, and pulled that for the rest of the afternoon. Kicker was on her mettle most of the time and we took care, as we didn't want any mistakes which would cause her to revert back to kicking, but all went well.

For the next two weeks she was given all the jobs we could find for her, carting dung, chain harrowing, snigging wood, until it was time for her to return home. I went with Father; we had a horse pulling the black trap and our friend Kicker following on.

When we arrived the owner said, 'How've you gone on with her?'

'Not too bad,' Father replied. 'She did think she was going to be boss. The only way to find out is to yoke her in that new cart over there.'

'Nay, we'll not do that,' he said, 'that cost me an arm and a leg. I'm not doing that, because I've seen what she can do. Will you do it and I'll hold your horse.'

Father and I yoked her to this new cart, took her to the midden and loaded up the cart with dung. We got the muck drag, a long shafted fork with prongs at right angles to the shaft, and went down the meadow, pulling heaps out every seven strides until it was empty.

Father walked back to the yard and I followed on, driving the horse, standing up in the cart. We had to go back through two narrow gates, over a bridge and into the yard, and she was as good as gold. We loosed her out and put her in the stable.

Father went for her owner to come and watch me taking off her harness and groom her in her stall. I groomed her by using the dandy brush, first on her neck, then her body and back legs. I had no fear, as I knew that I could trust her. Her owner was amazed at the change in this horse after a few weeks of firm handling, where never once had she been hit with either a whip or a stick.

To end this story, I must state that her real name was Rose which we thought appropriate as, at the beginning, she was really prickly! Rose worked on that farm for the next ten years, not causing any trouble. Her owner asked how we managed it, but Father just laughed and said, 'All she needed was firm handling.'

23

GINGER

Ginger was another difficult horse that Father was asked to take. One day he received a letter from a gentleman in the area, asking him to take a horse that he had bought for his daughter, June, who had been riding her in the hunt and other local equestrian events. Apparently, June had ridden the horse at the Bentham Agricultural Show, where her horse jumped the first round easily. When it came to the second round, however, June could tell her mood had changed and she refused fence number three. June tried her again and again and, on her last desperate attempt, the horse baulked in such a way that she threw June onto the poles, which resulted in a broken arm and fractured rib.

I wasn't there when Father received this letter, as I only visited my parents at the weekend, but I was to hear this story many times, and I was even to play some part in it. I will call the horse Ginger, as I cannot remember her pedigree name. As you can guess, she was ginger with dark legs and feet, and she was a beautiful animal.

Father arranged to collect Ginger at Mill Houses, equidistant from the farm and Wennington, where the horse lived. The man arrived in a high gig, with rubber rims on the wheels, and he had Ginger following on behind. It was a very nice turnout. Ginger's saddle and bridle were in the gig, as they had been specially made for her, so Father put them on her because he had no intention of walking home. He had had a lift there and he intended to ride back. The man cautioned Father and, at the same time, moved the gig well away.

Father mounted Ginger and she made every move possible to dislodge him. She bucked, reared and turned in the air, with her head between her front legs, and all this in a small area on the tarmac on which marks were left for days.

Whilst this was going on, a farmer and his wife from the nearby farm had been watching intently. The farmer's wife said, 'You must have glue between that saddle and yer breeches. It's not possible ter stay on like that wi'out!'

Father made his way home with a smile on

his face, not letting Ginger go faster than a canter. Reaching the first of the three gates that led to the farm, he thought, 'This horse is supposed to be able to jump, so now's her chance.'

Starting from about fifty yards away, he cantered towards the gate but she skidded to a halt when she got there, threw back her head and, in doing so, hit him in the face. This made Father determined not to be beaten and he took this horse, which had now got on the wrong side of him, back fifty yards to try again. He knew what to expect and this time, when Ginger slid to a halt, he had the crop ready in his hand and he hit her between the ears, with the silver ball on the end of it. This felled her instantly and, as she went down, he dismounted, hoping she wasn't injured.

After only a few seconds, Ginger was back on her feet. Father was back in the saddle as she arose, ready to try again. He took her back fifty yards, cantered forward and cleared the gate easily. There were two more gates for her to jump on the way home and, as she came to them, he waited for her to do her worst but she cleared each one with ease.

When Ginger had been put in her stall, groomed, fed, watered and bedded down,

Father looked at her and wondered how such a beautiful and, to all appearances, good-natured horse, could have behaved so badly.

Two days later, I was visiting my parents once more and I heard about this horse. I had to see her. 'Can I ride her?' I asked.

'Yes,' Father replied, 'as long as you don't let her break from a canter into a gallop. Now think on.'

I agreed, got on her back and went round the three-acre meadow about four times. Feeling confident, as I was a good rider, I decided that on the next time round I would let her have her head. Ginger felt the reins loosen and that was a signal for her to go into an unbelievable move, leaping into the air, twisting her body as she went and tucking her head between her legs as she came down. I had no alternative but to come off.

Now the horse had been newly-shod and, as she went over me, the heel of the hind shoe hooked into my eyebrow, leaving it hanging down in front of my eye. Blood was running down my face.

Father caught the horse and I went over to him. He put me straight back onto Ginger and said, 'You didn't do as I told you, now did you? Maybe this time you'll listen and do as you're told. Take the horse once round and then we'll take her in.'

Mother was there looking worried when I dismounted from the horse. I was taken inside, the wound was bathed, my eyebrow replaced carefully and a bandage put round my head, One thing that can be said about Mother is that she was an excellent nurse, and my eyebrow healed so well that all I can feel today is a small ridge in its hairline.

When Father made more enquiries about Ginger after this incident, he found that from being a foal she had always been treated with care. This made her wilful. June had let her have her own way too often. We soon found that she would try everything: in the stable she would cross over in front of you and, when fastened to the ring outside the stable door, she would pull back hoping to break the rope. She did many other things, too numerous to mention.

This was going to be a battle of wills and, knowing how good Father was with horses, this was going to be a testing time for Ginger. She was driven round in the paddock on a long rein, first clockwise and then anticlockwise. Even then, when she became bored, she would suddenly turn round to face the driver. After a few days of handling she improved, but she was not to be trusted.

Other work had to be done on the farm and then came Market Day, which gave Ginger a rest. Her owner was at Bentham; he enquired about her and, knowing her, he was not surprised at what Father had to tell. Father wanted to know how far the lessons could go to make Ginger a safe horse. They agreed that steps had to be taken to make her behave properly as the alternative was slaughter, and now Father wanted to win. When Ginger was next in training, she was going to find out what it was like to do exactly as she was told. I was not there at the time of this training, as I had gone back to Ingleton School, but my brother Nicholas was there and remembers it well.

Ginger was ridden for a while in a large, rough field, still trying her tricks. Then she was brought back near the stable, her saddle removed and replaced with a girth, which went over her back, behind the chine, round her body and behind her front legs. Two fetlock straps, with a ring at the back of each, were fastened on each front fetlock. A long rope was fastened to the ring on the girth, then taken to the ring on the far front leg, back to the girth, down to the near leg and back to the girth again. Mother held Ginger firmly whilst this was done.

Father took Ginger into the field and, holding the lunging rope along with the rope attached to her legs, he trotted her clockwise, gathering speed to a point where she thought of taking off. Father called out, 'Whoa, Ginger.' To Ginger's surprise, he pulled the rope attached to her front legs, taking her legs from under her, and down she went onto the soft ground. Travelling at speed, this was the biggest shock of her life but she rose, none the worse, and trotted clockwise a few more times.

She was then driven anti-clockwise and she must have thought, 'I've had enough of this.' She lurched from a slow walk into a full gallop. Father expected this, pulled her front legs from under her and down she went as the rope tightened when she reared. When she hit the ground, even though it was soft, she did a somersault and lay there winded. After a few minutes she was up again, her nostrils open with rage. Again Father drove her round, not pulling the rope from her legs. When the time came to stop her, Father called out again, 'Whoa Ginger!' and she stopped as soon as he spoke the words.

She was then harnessed into a cart used for breaking in horses. Two people sat on the cart, one holding the rein at one side and the other holding the rein at the other side. After a few jumps and bucks, she walked on and found the cart easy to pull. To find out how good she would be with a load, a chain harrow was fastened to the rear of the cart and, as she was so fit, she pulled it with no trouble.

After unyoking her, petting her all the time, she was groomed and fed in the stable, with everyone there praising her. Now Ginger was ridden over jumps, which took her back and forward over the stream in the meadow.

She was yoked in chains and in the shafts every day for two more weeks. When the time came to go to Bentham for groceries and to attend to other business, Mother and Father went with Ginger in the shafts of the black trap. The owner and his daughter were talking with friends outside the Brown Cow Inn when this horse came striding past, to be unharnessed and stabled behind the inn. They couldn't believe it, as they understood that the horse was only going to be trained for riding and even this was not going to be easy.

Father explained that when a horse is yoked in a cart or chains, she has to get used to being enclosed in harness with the shafts or chains rubbing against her. She has to pull when coming to a hill and hold back when going down hill.

A few weeks later, I was back at the farm and the time had come for Ginger to go back to Wennington. With Ginger in the shafts and her stable mate from our farm following behind, we set off feeling downhearted at seeing her go. When we arrived at her home, everyone was out to greet her.

'Will you ride her over the jumps to let us see how well she behaves?' asked June.

My Father said to me, 'Do you think you can manage? What you must do is take her round and let her look at each jump, as they are painted different colours.'

June was so taken with seeing her yoked in the trap that she wanted to drive her on the road first. This she did with her father; they went up the road a little way and came back, looking pleased. Then the saddle and bridle were put on Ginger and I was given a leg up. Riding into the field towards the jumps, Ginger made a noise through her nostrils at every other stride and I could tell she knew what was expected of her as she knew those jumps. I took her round a few times, making her walk, to let her see everything and, as she did the second round at a walk, I felt her relax. She went over the smaller jumps with ease, with June watching every move.

'Will you take her over the high jumps and the five-barred gate?' she called.

This I did and Ginger was brilliant. She sailed over each one and it seemed to please her. I then took her over the smaller jumps with her reins in a knot on her neck, using my legs to guide her. June was so delighted that she was laughing when she was talking to Father, but he looked at me, shook his head and said, 'You're a right show off. You were enjoying these people seeing you handle Ginger.'

Ginger won at many shows after that and Jane thought a lot about her, in spite of the accident.

24

1941: ANOTHER SPOILED HORSE

The stable was easy to find in nearly all farmyards because of the width of the door and the door itself. Most stable doors had a looped handle that made for easy opening with cold hands and with plenty of leverage to help with the opening whilst you were leading a horse. Many horses have been spoiled early in their working lives going in or out of the stable when fully harnessed for work with cart gear or trap harness, and with blinkers narrowing their vision. This was why Grandfather never allowed any of his horses, when they started their training, to be taken through the stable doorway wearing cart gear or trap harness. If the harness caught the door jamb, the horse would bolt forward, putting the person leading it in danger and maybe breaking the harness. It would also make the horse wary each time it went through the door. Many good horses were ruined through careless-ness.

This story is about one of Father's horses which he gave little money for as he knew her to have been 'spoiled', as we called it. When Father bought her, he paid the amount the abattoir would have paid. Father thought she was too good to be slaughtered and he liked a challenge. He must have been sure of success. Nicholas, my brother, was involved with this horse but only to open or close gates, or to fetch and carry.

The horse was harnessed outside the stable and a blindfold was added to the head collar. She was made to walk around until she had no idea where in the yard she was standing. The cart was close to the barn wall, leaving enough room for her to be yoked facing the wall. When the shafts were lowered and the chain, or back band as it was called, was in the groove on the saddle, all her muscles were taut, ready for escape. All the chains were fastened as quickly as possible, as was the belly band, and she calmed down. The cover over her eyes was carefully removed, then she was taken into the field and driven around with no trouble.

Back in the yard there was more to come. Once more the cover was put over her eyes and Father made sure she could not see out. He turned her first to the left and then to the right until she came to a halt, facing four feet away from the barn wall. A rope was fastened from her halter to a ring in the wall. Father told Nicholas to stand well away. The breaching chains were undone, the belly band taken off and then, carefully, the hame chains were unfastened. As the shafts were lifted clear, the horse lunged forward to escape, not realising that the barn wall was in her path. She ran into the wall with such force that she was dazed and bruised.

The rest of the day was spent yoking her to

the cart, taking her round the field, returning to the yard and, with the blindfold on, unyoking her until it was possible to lift the shafts off safely. After a week of careful handling and a lot of petting and kind words, it was possible to dispense with the blindfold. Father used her for much of the spring work and she settled down to be a reliable horse.

I never knew her name.

25

FARM SALE AT YARLSBER

When the farm sale at Yarlsber took place on September 27th, 1941 one horse was not sold. She was a Cleveland bay, with black legs and feet, no white anywhere, and she stood sixteen-hands three-inches high. She was seven years old and her name was Dinah. Grandfather had bought her from the Post Office, where her job had been to deliver parcels, pulling a four-wheeled dray.

There was a farm sale because Grandfather had decided to retire and Uncle

James did not want to farm. A place called Raber Top, with four acres of land, had been bought. It was ready for Grandfather to move into to live out his retirement. All the machinery and livestock, apart from Dinah, had been sold along with the small tools. The grazing of the land was sold in lots, to be grazed until March the following year. The turnips growing in Cemetery Meadow, along with thirty rows of mangles, all sold for around seventeen shillings per row, and were carted off for feed. All the hay and straw was sold, a bay at a time, and the buyer had to move most of it by horse and cart. The farmers in the area bought most of it; some was sold to the new owner of Yarlsber, so that stayed where it was.

Yarlsber was, and still is even after all these years, a place of many memories. I think back now and can picture the many things that happened when I was there, but I never thought at the time of leaving about how Grandfather must have felt.

The time soon came when the people moved out of Raber Top to live in the village and the place was vacant. The garden and building tools and short ladders had to be put by, together with many other odds and ends. These were not sold and had to be taken by horse and cart to the new home. This was my job.

Uncle James helped to load the cart, putting on what I thought were big loads, because ropes were used to fasten down anything above the cart sides. The best thing for me was that I would be driving this good-looking horse, yoked in a newly-painted cart, with the harness all polished and the brasses shining. I could drive down Back Gate and past Ingleton School in the hope that some of my mates would see me. After I passed the school, I went on past the new village and turned right up a lane to arrive at the yard in front of Raber Top.

The tools on the cart had to be put in a building at the top of a cobbled yard which was very steep. I thought that there was no way I could possibly back the load up such a steep slope. Carrying everything up there was the only thing possible and that was going to take me a long time. First I found a post long enough to scotch the two wheels at the entrance, and this I put at the side near the wall. I then led Dinah past the gate and turned her, with the back of the cart into the entrance, hoping she would be able to hold the cart whilst I put the post in front of the wheels to take the weight from her. To my

119

surprise, Dinah put back her ears and backed the loaded cart up that steep cobbled yard, right to the door where the load had to be taken off. She alarmed me with the speed at which she moved. I have never seen any horse that could back a load like her since then.

On my return I told Grandfather what had happened and he wasn't a bit surprised. He said, 'Dinah was used in a four-wheeled dray all the time she was working for the Post Office and she must have backed many a load into a difficult place.'

A few days later, Tommy Staveley parked his cattle truck, all nice and clean, near the steps in front of Yarlsber, ready to take the furniture the two or so miles to Raber Top. When all the rooms were empty, I was amazed at how large they looked, and how hollow they sounded as my aunts moved round making sure every room was spotless.

A week or so later, when the family was settled in the new home, the cart was loaded with spare tools together with things found in corners that had been missed when the sale took place. With Dinah, once more in the shafts, Grandfather said, 'Take this lot to your father's farm. He might find use for some of it.'

My parents lived six miles from Raber Top and, with the big horse taking long strides and me sitting comfortably on top of the load, the journey seemed to take no time. At the end of the track that led to the farm where my parents lived, a load of coal had been delivered just before I arrived. The driver gave me the delivery note and said, 'Tha's just landed right, lad. This job'll keep thi' oot o'bother for't rest o't day.'

Father, my younger brother Nicholas and my sister Jane all helped me offload the cart. I handed over the delivery note the man had given me to Father. 'Dinner's not ready yet,' he said. 'It'll be half an hour and, if we get a move on, we'll get a load of coal home in that time. The horse is already in the cart.'

Jane stayed home and the rest of us took shovels, rode down there and put a good load on the cart. We walked back to the farm so as not to add to Dinah's load. We were soon opposite the hole in the wall that had a door that opened outwards, which was already open. Father went into the house, whilst I turned Dinah so the back end of the cart was near the hole. I walked to the 'heck', or tailgate, to make the job easier. At that precise moment, when the heck was loose, Father walked past Dinah's head and must have touched her head collar. She thought this was the time she needed to back the cart. Immediately she went into reverse with her ears back. Luckily for me, the tailgate was on end in an up-and-down position, with the wide side between the cart and the wall, and this saved me from being crushed. Time seemed to slow down, even though it was only seconds, and I shouted, 'Let go of her!' whilst at the same time making a dive from behind the cart and falling on the ground.

I got to my feet and saw Father's white face. He was certain I had been badly injured but the tailgate had taken the pressure and saved my life. Good luck was on my side that day. As soon as Father had let go of Dinah, she had stopped.

Not much was said as I took Dinah to the stable and gave her some feed. Then we all had our meal, with Mother making all sorts of remarks about dangerous horses. After the meal, we fetched the rest of the coal, with Father staying well away from Dinah's head. Not only that, we removed the tailgate before the cart was near the bob hole; it was a lesson never forgotten.

I stayed the night, had breakfast next morning and then yoked Dinah in the cart.

We made our way back to Raber Top, with me once more enjoying the handling of this grand, big horse.

26

HIGH SCATHWAITE

After leaving school at fourteen, I spent about two years working for Uncle Robert on his farm at High Scathwaite. He had the same interest in horses as Grandfather, and he wanted only the best. Along with most farmers, he was told by the Ministry of Agriculture that a portion of the farm had to be ploughed. This was done with two horses pulling a two-wheeled cellar plough.

One day, when I had finished watering the young stock, cleaned the muck from the group, foddered them and made sure each one was fastened by its neck to either the boskin or the wall, Aunty Nellie had a basket and a can shaped like a small milk churn ready for me to take to Riggy Meadow, where Uncle Robert was ploughing. I waited not far from the gate, watching the two big horses coming towards me pulling the plough with no apparent effort. Behind the plough, the soil appeared like an endless ribbon.

The horses stood together, watching us eating our 'bagging' and drinking the coffee, interested each time we took a bite or a drink. The time this took was soon over and Uncle Robert said, 'Take hold of the reins. I'll hold the stilts. Turn into the furrow going the other way.'

Eager as I was to have a go, I knew this wasn't going to be as easy as it appeared to be. I turned the horses along the 'heading', which is the turning area at each end of the furrow, and made a botch of it because, by turning the two horses too soon, the plough was nowhere near the right place. This meant driving them in a figure of eight to start again, with orders to get it right this time. I hoped Uncle Robert would say when the plough was in the right place and he did, just as the mould board was parallel with the furrows. He then said, 'Turn them in,' and the plough was pulled into the correct position.

I was relieved that was over and handed over the reins. I watched again as the plough seemed to glide through the turf. I walked along with him and, when we reached the other end, he said, 'Take hold of the reins again. You'll never learn any younger.'

I managed much better this time but I thought there was no way I could drive the horses and handle the plough as he did. After many attempts at each end, I was sent off to do another job.

In the evening when the day's work was done, I told Aunty Nellie about my poor attempt at ploughing. She said, 'Robert thought you did quite well. He said he only needed to explain to you once. As in most things, it is practice and knack that is needed.'

I enjoyed the time I spent at High Scathwaite because I was treated well and continued to work with top-quality horses. Every time Uncle Robert went to a horse sale he took me with him. Horses of every type were taken to sell at Kendal Auction, and I spent every minute there listening to the comments made about them, not always in their favour. The horses were walked between two rows of buyers and onlookers, turned around and then made to trot away and back to let everyone see if they were sound in wind, limb and eyesight. Mr Hodgson, the auctioneer at the time, would try to make as much as possible for each horse, knowing the seller's livelihood partly depended on him.

Horses that didn't sell, not having reached the reserve, were taken home or maybe a buyer would try making an offer, starting at the refused price and bidding up bit by bit. At each bid he would hold out a hand, hoping the seller would slap it, which was a sign that he agreed to sell at the price offered. This bargaining could still be going on at the end of the sale. All kind of tricks would be used, such as pretending to walk away or saying, 'It's not really the horse I'm looking for.' Sometimes the buyer would feel down the horse's legs, saying, 'There's a lump here and here.' He would know there were no lumps.

As we travelled home, I asked why all this happened.

'It's called horse trading but pretending to find faults that aren't there isn't an honest way,' Uncle Robert explained. 'I'm glad you saw that.'

A blue Fordson Major tractor was in the yard when we arrived home. It belonged to a contractor and behind it was a two-furrow plough on wheels. He had come to plough a very steep field, above the house to the west. Uncle Robert went with him to show him the field, whilst I did the jobs around the farm. That evening we told Aunty Nellie all that had gone on at Kendal, as we sat round the table having our meal.

The contractor came back the next day to plough the field, as he had only had time to mark out the area to be ploughed the previous day. Again Uncle Robert went with him, whilst I worked in the yard. When dinner time came Aunty Nellie and I waited for what seemed to be forever before eating our meal, and still Uncle Robert did not come back. We wondered what had happened to him.

I went up the track to see where he was, only to find the tractor on its wheels in the meadow beyond the fence, with the exhaust and air filter bent over the tank. The plough was on its side in the field, which was half-ploughed. Uncle Robert and the contractor were sitting smoking.

As I walked towards them, I couldn't decide whether or not to tell them dinner was on the table, but they knew. We all walked home, not saying a word. They had their meal, whilst I stayed outside, doing a job and wondering what had happened. I could tell whatever it was must have been serious but, as I have said before, Uncle Robert was always calm in a crisis. They took some tools back to the tractor with them to repair the damage, and some time later I heard the tractor start up.

That evening I was told everything. The tractor, whilst turning on the steep slope, had rolled over four times and gone through the hedge into the field. The driver had managed to jump off and had run down the hill trying to turn left, out of the path of the oncoming tractor. All the time he was struggling to keep on his feet and he only got clear as the tractor rolled through into the next field. What he couldn't know at the time was that the plough had been left behind. Had that not happened, he would have been killed.

Uncle Robert said, 'Give me horses every time!'

27

HIGHER SALTER

I had now passed my sixteenth birthday and was very happy living at High Scathwaite. One morning, when we were having breakfast, the postman came with a letter for Uncle Robert. I recognised Mother's writing. It told him that I had to go home, as Father had taken over a large fell farm at the top end of Roeburndale, with a large flock of sheep. I was needed to help them move, lock, stock and barrel from the farm in Tatham Fells to High Salter. I had no choice.

One day, Father arrived home after attending one of the last horse sales at Kendal Auction Mart. He told us who he had seen and all the news, as there were no telephones in the homes, as there are today. We all listened with interest, waiting for him to mention any dealings he might have had. Most times, he would leave home saying, 'I've no intention of buying any horses.' This occasion being no exception, we were surprised when we asked if he had bought a horse to be told, 'Yes and no.'

What happened was that one of the auction staff brought out a horse to sell as the owner was not able to attend, and there was no information available about it. Therefore this horse had to be bought as seen, with no guarantee. No one made a bid, even after it had been trotted back and forth many times. The auctioneer, Mr Hodgson, did his best, starting at a price and dropping all the time. At last he said, 'This horse is far too good to be sent for fat.'

Knowing Father as he did, he knocked the horse down to him. Father followed the horse back to its stable to find out what he had acquired for such a low price. Later he paid for her and the Auction Mart Company agreed to make all the arrangements to send her by train from Kendal to Hornby, arriving there about six p.m. I knew what was coming – a job for me.

Father said, 'I'll take you in the car to the station and you can lead her home.'

As I did not want to walk the six miles home, it was agreed that I would ride one of the horses we had at the time, and bring this new horse home on a lead rein. I was soon on my way after closing the gate across the road at Middle Salter.

Mr Woodhead, from just inside the doorway of the woodshed, said, 'Is tu' going courtin' on horseback?'

'Not this time,' I replied, with a laugh.

I was pleased when the porter led the new horse out of the horsebox. He passed the halter shank up to me, just as she came near my right-hand side. He said, 'This one's a live wire!'

Being strangers, both horses had their ears forward and were showing the whites of their eyes because each was wary of the other. By the time we had travelled halfway home, they were becoming friendly. I had no problems. I could tell by the way the new horse moved that she was very different from any I had handled before. What held my interest was the way she walked and, even more so, the way she trotted.

Nicholas had our gate open, so I would not need to dismount until I arrived back home. He was eager to see the new horse, not knowing what to expect after being told how she had been knocked down to Father. A stall had been bedded with straw. Feed was in the manger and hay in the rack. Father led her to the water trough, but did not let her drink much as she would be watered again later. As she stood in the stall, I knew that this was a real bargain.

She was a dark bay, fifteen-and-a-half hands, with black legs and feet, black mane and tail, long ears, and no white anywhere. Best of all, she had kind eyes.

Father said, 'What do you think of her?'

My reply was, 'There's more to this horse than we think.'

The farm work went on as usual, attending to the cows and young stock and then walking most of the day checking the sheep. Meanwhile the four horses were in different fields and brought in at night, until we had some spare time. We decided that this horse had to be yoked into the breaking harness to see what she was capable of, and care was taken as she was put between the shafts. All went well. Father held the reins, sitting on the cart, whilst I held a long leading rein and walked, holding it near her head, not knowing what to expect. It wasn't long before she settled and the lead rein was taken off. She behaved so well, we knew she was fully broken.

After dinner, as we called it then, a few groceries were needed from Wray. A saddle was put on this horse with no name, and I was to find out if she had ever been ridden.

I had the bag for the groceries on my back and I mounted with care. All the way to Wray I let her walk, as her movements were so quick; every other stride, I could hear a snort as she let out a breath. The journey passed quickly as I was watching everything this horse did, not knowing what she might do next.

Mr Newton saw me outside his shop and came to see what I needed. When the few things were packed into the backpack, he helped me put it on. The journey home was mostly uphill and I thought this would make her easier to handle. Not so; like all horses she knew she was making for home. On the level I let her have her head a little, still wary, because I couldn't rise and fall in the saddle when her action was so new to me. The best I could do was to sit firm and lean back and that worked.

I made her walk up Dick Hill and the next hill, but before the gateway onto Whitmore this dark bay horse was determined to have her head. I could see that holding her back was beginning to upset her. I talked to her and patted her neck, with no effect. The only way was to gradually ease my hold on the reins. This was when I got the shock of my life. This was no ordinary horse. Whoever had owned her had trained her to be a pacer and, because the two legs on each side moved forward together, this made her so different to ride. She opened out, covering the ground at such speed I wondered however she could keep on her feet and whether I would be able to slow her down before going down Barkin Gate. Thankfully she slowed to a walk and calmed down when we got there, then walked steadily the rest of the way. She was soon in the stable, unsaddled, brushed down and fed.

Father wanted to know how she had behaved. I told him and I could tell that he thought I was exaggerating, especially when I said, 'This is the fastest horse I have ever had any dealings with.'

A week later, two men came into the yard, having heard about this horse and wanting to buy her. She was yoked in a light gig and taken into the big meadow. I took her twice round the flat area, not letting her open out, hoping they would lose interest in buying her. I drove home, unyoked her, taking off her harness in her stall, just as Father and the men came through the door.

Each man looked her over in turn. I knew then that there was no way they could be put off, even though Father had put a high price on her and would take no less. It was arranged that a lorry would come for her next day. They paid cash there in the stable and Father gave them half-a-crown for luck. They wanted the horse to be kept inside in her stall, and one of them said, 'Don't let her come to any harm.'

I was always sorry to see any horse leave, even when I knew it would be well cared for. We were still interested in this horse with no name and Father asked his friends about her when he went into Lancaster. He would ask if they could tell him what she was doing, but he heard nothing for two years until one day when he was in a conversation at Lancaster Auction. Apparently the men had found out about her breeding before coming to the farm and that was the reason they were so determined to have her. Since then she had won many trotting or harness races for them.

When he came home and told us this, all I could say was, 'I did tell you she was the fastest horse I had ever ridden.'

28

WARTIME AT HIGHER SALTER

Higher Salter was being used by the armed forces for their training when we went there. The soldiers from the Royal Enniskillen Fusiliers came every day and, because of them, our workload was far greater. Each day we were told which area they would use for target practice and, as they used live ammunition, 303 rifles, trench mortar shells and machine guns, all the sheep had to be moved out of range. Father would leave me to feed and water the cattle and horses during the winter time, and take two dogs onto the High Close, to gather the sheep and take them over White Bank, out of the firing line. Many unexpected things happened, far too many to write about, but here are some of them.

There had been a usable track from Higher Salter over White Bank and on through Mill Race to Slaidburn, but the army vehicles changed that. About nine o'clock each morning we could see the convoy of vehicles coming down 'Barkin'. First, there were three Willis jeeps and up to fifteen trucks full of soldiers, followed by Bren gun carriers and half-track vehicles. These caused the damage, as they churned up the road surface so badly that even the army couldn't use it.

When spring came, the job of moving the sheep was handed over to me. Soon it was lambing time and the sheep were brought inland off the fell, making sure that none were left behind.

One back end was very wet and the army was there on manoeuvres. The soldiers were learning map reading with a compass. They were given a route to follow and were dispatched at intervals. I was shepherding on White Bank and could see soldiers going in all directions. Later, I came across five who were lost.

'Where are you making for?' I asked.

They handed me the map and pointed to Abbeystead.

'You're going in the wrong direction,' I said.

'How do you know?' said one of the men.

'I'm a shepherd, so I know the area well,' I replied.

I spent some time showing them how to

use the map and found they had no idea what contour lines were and didn't know how to use a compass.

'Make your way up there and then look down the valley to your right,' I said, 'and if all else fails, follow the stream. Water always runs downhill.'

Later, one of the officers told Father, 'It was like they had been given orders to go in different directions. It was twenty-four hours before they were all accounted for.'

Another time, the rain was so heavy the soldiers looked like drowned rats. They were wet to the skin. We felt sorry for them and so Father sent me to ask the officer to come to see him. When he came, Father told him to use the turf house for a cookhouse and the lads could use one of the empty barns across the green for shelter, as they were staying overnight.

We had about twenty hens in a loosebox near the house, so we made sure the doors were well fastened but not locked. We were pleased to find all the hens were there next morning. We saw the men given a hot meal around noon. They all lined up with their billycans near the turf house and ate the food in the shelter of the barn.

Our meal was ready later and we took

longer to eat it, as we could hear the army vehicles pulling out. We went back to work when all was quiet. We looked around to see what damage had been done. We found doors open, gates unfastened and hay all over the barn floor, trampled down and dirty.

'Well at least they were out of the rain, poor lads,' said Father.

The Fusiliers moved on and the American soldiers came. They only stayed for a short time compared to the Fusiliers. Soon after they arrived, Father moved the sheep away from their training area, as he had done before. He stood for a while on White Bank, watching about ten Bren gun carriers lining up on the low side of the track in the High Close, wondering what they hoped to do. When he got back to where the men in charge were standing, he asked the officer what they intended.

The Officer said, 'It is not your concern. This is army business. Thank you for moving the sheep.'

Father said, 'There's no way those vehicles will go more than fifty yards.'

The man turned round and said angrily, 'Keep your opinions to yourself.'

Father stood silently by, knowing what

would happen. The sergeant ordered them to get into line and gave the signal to advance. Three carriers on firmer ground got ahead whilst the others, on peaty ground, made much slower progress. With their engines at full throttle, the tracks were digging many feet deep into the soft peat. They were not aware that ahead of them was a bog they couldn't avoid. As the three leading carriers reached the edge of the bog, their front ends dipped immediately and this caused alarm, as their exit hatches were close to the bog level.

When everyone was standing on firm ground, Father started to walk towards home. When he was about to close the gate between the two big fields, a jeep caught up with him. The officer walked over to ask his advice, as he had no idea how to save the three carriers from sinking into the bog. Father could see he was embarrassed about what he had said earlier, so he climbed into the jeep with his dogs and went back with them. His first piece of advice was to fasten a carrier to the back of each of the sinking carriers using a heavy chain to stop them sinking any deeper, and so using the carrier on firm ground as an anchor. The officer listened keenly to everything he advised.

'You must use minimum revs in low gear as you do this, so that the sward will be left unbroken. Then there is a chance no more will get bogged down,' Father said.

When the three in the bog were anchored at last, it was well past dinner time and Father told them he was going home. Before he went, he said, 'Use the metal posts on that truck to make a road. That will give a grip for the anchor carriers and stop them sinking if the sward gets broken.'

The officer said, 'We'll send you home in the jeep and the driver will wait for you, if you will agree to come back.'

When they returned, the men had eaten and were keen to start. Father was in charge. Two more carriers were coupled in line with heavy towing chains in front of the first anchor. The track of posts was already down for them to make the first critical pull and Father stressed again that the engine revs must be at their lowest and they must all pull together and stop when told.

When the first carrier was finally out, they had to do the same thing all over again. First the posts had to be moved for the two carriers to stand on. They got the second one out, but only just, as one of the drivers started to rev his engine and this was pulling the sward and posts back with his vehicle tracks. The sergeant shouted a lot of choice words at him, when he ordered him to take his foot off the throttle.

The last of the three was impossible to move. It was going dusk so, after much discussion, it was left as it was, with a carrier for an anchor.

Next day a large eight-wheeled truck with a winch came and was there most of the day. They had it out by the afternoon but, as the engine had been under water, it had to be towed back to the barracks.

The officer called to thank Father for his help and advice, and gave him some petrol, as this was the only thing he had to give.

Father said, 'I'm just glad to know that all the carriers are safe.'

Another time two unexploded bombs, dropped by enemy aircraft in Low Close, had to be dealt with. We were warned that they would be exploded at eleven a.m. and any glassware or pictures should be moved to safety. My sister Jane was in bed with flu at the time, and all Mother could think to tell her was to put her head under the pillow, ready for the bang. We had heard so much gunfire by then that Father, Nicholas and I

142

went on with our work, as usual. When eleven o'clock came the explosion was a shock to all of us. I felt as though my eardrums had burst.

Father said, 'No wonder that fellow came to warn us.'

All the chimneys had slates propped on them as a reverse 'V' and not one stood the shock. We also heard a lot of noise coming from inside the house and went in to investigate, wondering what had happened. We found that more than half the ceiling in Jane's room had fallen, most of it onto the bed. We moved the biggest pieces off and, as we lifted the piece from the pillow she had over her face, Jane said, 'I thought the whole roof had fallen in!'

Thankfully, she was none the worse.

29

THE AMERICAN ARMY

We had found farming difficult during the time our soldiers were doing their training at Higher Salter, but we soon realised the difference when the American unit came towards the end of the war. They had more of everything: food, petrol, vehicles, artillery and ammunition.

When Father asked their officer to see the gates were closed after they passed through, he was told that it was his job to close them if he wanted them closed. Didn't he realise there was a war on? Father came back to tell us what had been said, and it was decided to fasten the road gates open because, he said, 'This lot are so arrogant that they will drive through the wooden gates if they are closed.'

The sheep were moved out of range early the next day. The fact that we could hear the engines revving up and the shouting of orders so near to the house was new to us, as this had never happened with the Enniskillen Fusiliers. All day long the guns and large artillery were going off, far worse than we were used to. Thankfully, they only came for six days and went back to the barracks each night, as the damage they did was worse than any the British lads had caused during their long training sessions.

It is said, 'You can always recognise a farmer as he always walks with his eyes on the ground.' The reason for this is because of what he might step in. Our reason was the same because there were so many unexploded shells and hand grenades outside the normal practice ground. When we found shells, we left markers near them. When the Americans had gone, Father and I found 303 brass rifle bullets in batches of fifty or more, grenades, mortar bombs and other things we had not seen before.

There was so much that we sent in a request to the army for a bomb squad to come and clear the area. Two jeeps arrived, each with a driver and a bomb disposal expert. They called at the farm with a map so we could point out where all these things were. Knowing their job would be difficult as they had not been here before, Father volunteered my services for the day. For no pay, I might add.

When it was going dusk that first day, they had found and exploded a lot more than we had seen. One of the men said, 'We have picked up enough live ammunition to start another war.' They could not believe how much they had found and had to come for more than a week with more men to make a reasonable job of it. Even then, we had to send in more reports.

Whilst the Americans were there, another incident occurred on about the fifth day. Father took his dogs, as usual, to move the sheep away from the training area as we had no information about the army's plans. Spring work was in full swing at home. We were busy carting dung with horses from near the buildings, and setting between eight and ten heaps per load in rows on the meadow, to be spread by fork as soon as possible.

When Father came late to the dinner table, we knew at once something was wrong. His face was white and the muscles on his jaw were taut. He said nothing.

We knew the best thing to do was to leave him alone. When he joined us outside later, we were told to take a spade each to the top end of High Close to bury twenty-two young lambs, which the Americans had shot for target practice. Some had taken hours to die as they had been shot through the gut. When a claim was made for these dead lambs, we had to dig them up to prove that they had been shot, because this had not happened before when our lads were training. I remember the men's faces when the first lambs were lifted out of the grave.

One of them said, 'Stop digging. We've seen enough.'

'No,' I replied. 'You're going to see all of them. There will be no mistake made.'

We pointed out to them that the twelve

female lambs would have been replacement stock, and the male lambs would have been sold at market in the back end of the year. This was our income. When the lambs were back in the ground and covered up, we asked them to inspect the damage to the boundary walls, so that when a claim was sent in they would have some idea what had really happened. They could tell that most of the gaps in the stone walls were new by the newly-broken stones and the fact that the craters, made by the shells, were not yet filled with water.

Nicholas and I, with help from another man, spent many hours repairing those walls. When I think back, I wonder however we had the will to start. The worst shock was when the cheque for the damage came from the War Department. The lambs were valued as new lambs and the damage to the walls was assessed as unavoidable. The compensation, therefore, was an insult. When remarks were made by others about the money that was being paid by the War Department for all those hours we spent repairing the walls, we said nothing. To make others believe the truth was a waste of time. Only those with experience will understand.

There was one further incident concerning the American soldiers. On their final day at Higher Salter Father had gone, as usual, to move the ewes and their lambs out of range of the guns. He made sure to move them all out of sight over White Bank, with the hill between the guns and the flock of ewes and lambs, hoping they would not make their way back before the guns stopped firing for the day. He checked the sheep over to the boundary fence and Wolfhole Cragg, and on the way back he gave them another push with his dogs to make sure. He then made his way back along the track towards home, and sat down behind a big stone on the highest point of White Bank to eat the food he had taken with him. The big stone gave good shelter from the wind and many shepherds will have sat behind it.

Nell, one of Father's dogs and his favourite, sat watching every mouthful as Father ate his sandwiches, hoping he would give a crust to her. She was a 'beardy', with long hair covering her eyes, and she would hold her head on one side so that she could see through her fringe. She knew no one could refuse her. Father threw the sandwich with the most crust a few feet away from the shelter of the big stone, and Nell raced to get it before the other dog. Father heard a 'zap' as she got to the crust, and she came back with her tail tucked in. Father sat for a while and checked Nell to see she was none the worse. He knew a shot had been fired.

He stood up to see what the Americans were doing as he knew the firing range was into the side of Mallowdale Pike, at right angles to where he was standing. All was still quiet, and he decided that now was the time to make his way home. The firing started again, but he could see they were pointing their guns towards the targets. When his trilby was pulled off his head he was shocked, knowing the wind couldn't be responsible. The dogs came back close to him when he sat down again; they knew something was wrong. When he thought about what had happened, he could not believe it. He went to collect his trilby from about thirty yards away and found two holes through the crown.

The firing had stopped for the day when Father walked up to the officer-in-charge to tell him what he thought of his management of his soldiers. He said, 'I would like to meet the soldier who wasn't firing at the target but was firing at me and my dogs.'

He showed the officer his hat with two holes through the crown and the officer laughed, which was a mistake. Father hit him square on his chin with his hard knuckles, and the man went down on the hard road. He made no attempt to get up as Father stood over him. No one interfered. Calling his dogs, Father walked away, not even turning to see what they would do next.

Once home, he told us his story. We were sitting in the living kitchen, having a drink and listening to him, when a jeep drew up outside. Not knowing what to expect, I answered the knock on the door to find an officer standing there.

'Can I have a word with the farmer, please?' he asked.

I asked him in but he refused, as time was short. Father came to the door and was given one hundredweight of sugar, two boxes of dried fruit and some cans of petrol, along with an apology.

That was the last we saw of the Americans.

30

A STORY FROM THE PAST

This is a story about Tommy who, when he was fifteen years old, was hired on as a 'dogsbody' at Winder Farm. The nearest village was Caton, nearly six miles down the valley of Littledale. Harvest Festival was held at the chapel not far from Littledale Hall, three miles away, and this was the subject being discussed at mealtimes, prior to the occasion. Church or chapel were the only places where people got together in their best outfits to meet and make friends.

Tommy hoped to go and asked his boss if it would be alright, as he would like to meet some of the young people that would be there. It was agreed that Tommy could go, as long as he made himself look respectable. This worried Tommy because he hadn't a posh suit, only the clothes he wore every day and a pair of trousers, a shirt and a jacket to change into while his other clothes were being washed.

The day of the Harvest Festival arrived. Tommy came in for breakfast, sat at the table not saying a word and looking very unhappy. When asked what was wrong, Tommy told them. He couldn't go as the clothes he had were only fit to wear on the farm.

The farmer's wife said, 'I have washed your trousers, shirt and jacket. I know they are well worn but they are clean.'

Tommy thanked her, finished his meal and went back to work. The farmer's wife knew Tommy had decided to stay at home because he was new in the area and some of the locals would make fun of him if he went in his old clothes.

The midday meal was now on the table, with Tommy eating his food and not saying anything that wasn't necessary. He was asked to go upstairs to make sure the clothes that had been washed and ironed looked better for it, and then decide. He found, set out on his bed, a suit, a shirt and stockings, not new but of good quality.

Tommy thought there was some mistake; these clothes could not be for him. He closed the door to his room and went down the stairs, to be told that they were now his to wear when he went anywhere special. Tommy couldn't think of anything to say.

His boss told him to get changed or the Harvest Festival would be over.

When Tommy reached the next farm, the farmer, his wife and their two daughters were going through the gate at the far end of the yard on their way to the chapel, so Tommy went along with them. On the way, they told Tommy that their farm was haunted. Every foggy night, a white horse could be seen moving across the field they were in then disappeared into the mist without a trace. Tommy listened in silence, not believing a word.

Apparently, two men with a white horse had been seen near places where robberies had been carried out. The robbers knew that when the draft ewes were sold at the sheep fairs, along with the wether lambs and wool, the farmers were paid in the coin of the day. Each farmer would then have this money ready to pay his rent, clear all his debts and have sufficient left over to keep his family for another year. He would hide it and use it as needed. One farmer had been given a description of the robbers by a neighbour and he warned his family to be on their guard when he and his brother were away.

The two brothers had gone shepherding, leaving their wives busy rendering the fat from the pig which they had butchered the previous day. There was a knock on the door. The older of the two women answered the door and she knew at once that the two men standing on the doorstep were the same men that they had been talking about. The big, unshaven man, with a mark on his left cheek, demanded food as they hadn't eaten for two days. The shorter, thickset man kept a lookout. Having been warned about them, and knowing these men were dangerous, she let them in out of the cold and fed them with a big bowl of hotpot left over from the midday meal. When they'd eaten the hot food, the men sat comfortably near the big fire and fell asleep.

Hoping their husbands would return soon, the two women carried on rendering the fat in the hot oven. They avoided the men's feet, especially when they were carrying the hot fat. The two men woke with a start just as the boiling fat was being taken out of the oven. The women were holding a tray each and passing one to the other, as they had done all the time the men were asleep. Hearing the men wake, the women turned in fear of what they were doing and the boiling fat and the hot tray hit each man in the face. The women were in shock, seeing these men in agony, knowing this had not been their intention.

The husbands arrived home to find their wives in a terrible state, doing all they could to ease the pain of the two men. They could see at once that there was no hope for either man. One of the brothers ran to the Hall to relate what had happened and get some help and advice.

With the help of their neighbours, the two robbers were buried in the paddock. The horse was seen in the field by the people who came to help. Next day, the two brothers went to see if it needed its harness removing and if there was something that would help to identify its owners, but the white horse was nowhere to be found.

Tommy lagged behind the others on the way back from the Harvest Festival, as the two sisters were being escorted home and their parents had already gone. Tommy fell back, thinking it was not going to be easy for him to make new friends because everyone was older or much younger than he was.

The mist was now covering the field he had walked through earlier. Tommy was taking care to keep to the path because he didn't want to lose his way. To his horror, he saw a white horse standing to his left. When it saw him it galloped away into the mist. Tommy, now terrified, ran and overtook the other people who were well ahead of him. He jumped the gates at each end of the farmyard, not slowing down until he arrived at the back door at Winder Farm. Leaving the door wide open, he ran up to his room and got into his bed, still wearing all his clothes and his boots. Hearing Tommy making such a racket, the farmer and his wife went to see what was wrong. They were worried and wondered what could have happened to put him in such a state.

When Tommy calmed down, he told them all that had happened, only to be told that the people who now lived at that farm had a white horse!

31

LEARNING TO WORK A SHEEPDOG

When my parents moved to Higher Salter, a large sheep farm at the top end of Roeburndale, I had to leave High Scathwaite to go to work there. This was where my education in working sheepdogs began.

One day, Nicholas and I were in the back meadow where Nicholas was running his young dog. We thought he was doing quite well. Now Bill Huddleston had come to visit that day. He had been the manager for Mr Taylor, the previous tenant at Higher Salter, and he was well known as an experienced dog handler. We were so busy watching this young dog at work that we didn't notice Bill standing behind us. When the dog came back, Nicholas was pleased with her and thought he had done well.

Bill said, 'It's a wonder you haven't sent that dog mad.'

Nicholas asked, 'Why? What have I done?' He was a bit shocked by Bill's comment.

Bill went on, 'Don't you realise that one command for everything you want that dog to do is no good? All I'm trying to tell you is that you need a command for clockwise around the sheep and a different command for anti-clockwise. Then you need a different command for fetch and drive away, as well as a stop command.'

We listened to him, taking in all he said, knowing how right he was. Bill said, 'If that dog is half a mile from you, how on earth can you make her change direction with only one command?'

157

We knew what he meant. Better still, he said, 'Let's catch up with those sheep and I'll see if this dog will take any notice of me.'

Nicholas and I stood watching Bill get Moss to go left around the sheep then stop her with a whistle and send her round to the right, before stopping her again. What amazed us most was that he seemed to control Moss with little or no effort.

From that short lesson, we took time out after work or on Sundays to tootle about with our dogs. This became our number one hobby, as shepherding was our main job of work, after the cows and young stock.

I had a dog called Jet at the time. She was black, with white neck and legs, and she was built for speed. I bought her from Fred Exelby, a family friend, and also a very keen dog handler. As I watched Fred work Jet on the day I bought her, I was amazed. I couldn't really understand how he could make her be at the right place at the right time. I worked Jet a few times and couldn't get her to respond in the way I had seen her respond to Fred. I thought at the time that I had wasted £20 of hard-earned cash.

Now most shepherds have their own commands. Some use voice, with 'come bye' for left, and 'away to me' or 'away here' for right.

They use 'walk on' for fetch and drive, and 'stand' for stop. Others use whistles, and both Nicholas and I learnt the whistles Bill Huddleston used. To do this we made marks on each hand to remind us, and then we could be sure not to confuse the dog. After a short time Jet got used to these whistles, which were different from the whistles that had been used in her earlier training. Each time I took Jet shepherding up High Close and then on to the Iron Gate, she got to know my commands.

When I stopped to eat the food I carried in my shoulder bag, Jet sat opposite me watching every mouthful, knowing I would give her some. I soon realised that the only way a dog can have enough energy for a long day's work was to let her do only what was necessary, and not to let the dog return to heel each time when sent a long way out. I had to stop the dog when she was at a distance, not let her return, and so cover the same ground twice. Instead, I made the dog wait until I had walked on, keeping watch on her, and then I gave the command to make the sheep move forward. When two dogs were gathering, one dog on the shepherd's left and the other on his right, large areas were gathered in one push.

32

SPY: ANOTHER SHEEPDOG

One evening after work, I cycled to see Bill Huddleston. He and his wife Olive were on their first farm between Mill Houses and Wennington. When I arrived Bill had just about finished his farm work for the day, with only the dogs to feed. Olive came to the door to tell him the evening meal was ready, so we went into the house.

When he had washed his hands, Bill said, 'Come and wash your hands. Olive has made enough food for all of us because she saw you coming up the track.'

During the meal the conversation was mostly about Higher Salter, as they had lived and farmed there before Father took over the tenancy. As soon as the meal was over Bill said, 'We'll take that young dog I've just bought to see if she is any good.'

The little bitch was called Spy and she was black, with a thin white mark down between her eyes to the end of her nose and one white front foot. On our way to the field, where there were about ten shearlings, I could see how keen she was to be at work. When we were in the field, not far from the sheep, Bill took off the lead. Instead of going at the sheep at speed, Spy went to the right, or anti-clockwise. At the same time, Bill went clockwise, around the sheep.

I looked on in amazement as I was just a novice with dogs, while Bill and his brothers were top class men at sheepdog trials. When Spy was on her lead and we had gone out of the field and along by the hedge for about fifty yards, she got loose. She went back to the gateway and crawled under it to go round the sheep again. Bill and I watched in amazement because she didn't try to bring them towards us but drove them back to the gate, which I had opened. She brought them through and turned them along the hedge to where we were standing. I couldn't believe it when Bill said, 'Spy has only been loose amongst sheep in the yard before when they needed attention.'

I had given up hope of buying her, as I could see that she was going to be more than I could afford. We talked for about ten minutes and, in the end, I plucked up the courage to ask if Spy was for sale, expecting the reply to be no. We went back to the house; it was getting chilly and dark. Olive made a drink and insisted I had a sandwich, as I had about seven miles to cycle home. When the time came to leave, which was later than I intended as I enjoyed their hospitality, Bill said, 'Come to see us again next week and we'll give Spy another run.'

I said, 'I would like to see her work sheep again, but I don't think I could afford her price.'

As I rode down the hills and on the level, the only thing on my mind was how well Spy handled those sheep. I didn't even notice the steep hills from Wray because I had enjoyed the visit.

A week later, when the day's work was done at home, I cycled down past Middle Salter and over the bridge. I walked up Barkin, which is a one-in-four steep hill, and rode the rest of the way without needing to dismount, as the journey was downhill or on the level. All the time I was wondering if I would be able to afford the price Bill would want for Spy.

This time I arrived much later to find, as I had hoped, that their evening meal was over. Even so, Olive handed me a mug of tea and a newly-baked scone on a plate, saying,

'We thought you would be here for the evening meal.'

I thanked them both and said, 'I have been thinking about it all week and there is no way that I could afford her.'

Bill got up from the table and said, 'Now you're here, we might as well take her out. She might not even look at the sheep this time.'

As we walked to the field with Spy on a lead, he said, 'I've been busy this week. Spy hasn't been off her chain so don't expect her to do as well. She may even chase them all over the place.'

I didn't think that this would happen. Off she went as before, moving all the time with her head down, showing just a bit of eye. Bill, as he did the last time, made his way to the right, or clockwise, to turn Spy back the way she had just come and then made her stop.

I couldn't take my eyes off them, trying to learn as much as possible, hoping that one day I would be able to run a dog as well as Bill. On the way back to the house, I asked him how much he wanted for her, still thinking the price would be more than I could afford. Lucky for me, Bill had two more young dogs that someone needed him to finish breaking in. He told me the price of

Spy, which was not nearly as high as I had expected, and he said, 'The only reason she is for sale is because I know you will get the best out of her and, at the moment, I have these others that need all my spare time.'

With my cycle and Spy in his Ford van, Bill drove us above halfway to Higher Salter to drop us off on Whit Moor. He turned his van round and was out of sight before I got sorted out with my bike in one hand and Spy's lead in the other. To my horror, she dived between my legs and was gone. All I could do was call her name. As it was getting dark I knew something had to be done as soon as possible.

I cycled back the four miles to get Bill to come, and hoped Spy would be near enough to hear his whistles. I arrived in the yard just as Bill was putting his van away. He couldn't believe that I was standing there so soon and knew immediately what had happened. Without saying a word, we made our way back to Whit Moor, both worrying and hoping Spy hadn't moved too far away out of calling distance. To our surprise, as soon as we were out of the van there she was, making a fuss of Bill. He thought she must have recognised the sound of the van, as her kennel was close to the garage.

I said, 'I can't thank you enough. I'm sorry for what has happened.'

Bill said, 'Thank goodness she knew the sound of the van. You will have to take more care this time.'

As expected, it took Spy some time to settle. Two weeks later, we had some sheep in the yard where we were sorting out twenty to go back to the fell. This was the first time Spy showed any interest. I had Father's dog, Nell, helping to take the twenty sheep to the fell. I knew what a good work dog she was and that we would get the job done.

Halfway across High Close I let Spy off the lead, wondering if she would stay with me. She moved away to the side of the sheep. Nell was at the other side, letting the sheep travel between them, with me following along behind.

When the sheep were through the gate, I put Spy on the lead to make sure she would stay with me and did not return to the sheep we had just left. The distance from the fell gate to home was over one mile. Halfway I let Spy loose with her lead trailing, hoping this would slow her down and make it possible for me to catch her if she didn't want to stay. Nell saw she was loose and started to play. This was the best thing that could have happened. I removed the lead from Spy's collar so that she was free to move without getting tangled in the rope.

Each night and on Sundays, when the work was done, I enjoyed training her in the front meadow. I would often go to see Bill, hoping he would take out a young dog to train because at the same time he would be training me. I was now very interested in learning the art of training sheepdogs properly.

33

TRIM: A DOG WORTH A MENTION

I took time off to go to Lowgill Sheep Dog Trials which were held once a year. The sports were on at the same time, making it an annual event that has continued every year till the present day. This was a popular event where as many as eighty sheep dogs were entered, with some contestants entering three dogs. I looked forward to it as it was a chance to watch the top handlers compete against each other and to make my choice as to which dog I could work with on the fell at Higher Salter.

The time came for the novice dogs to show what they could do. A 'novice' is a dog or bitch that has not won a first prize. These young dogs were putting on a very good show and it was easy to see that their owners had spent many hours training them.

My friend Bill Huddleston's turn came to run his young dog, Trim, a big black dog. The only white on him was on his left front foot, like a short sock. Trim really let his master down. He set off to gather his sheep from Bill's right, to begin his outrun to pick up the five young animals. As soon as he had to pass some of the onlookers, he sat down in an upright position with his ears up and stayed there until Bill put on his lead to take him back to his van.

I went across to find out what could have happened to make a dog stop like he did. Many of Bill's other friends came over to pass their opinions, as they had seen Trim practising at home. They decided that either one of the onlookers had done something that had terrified him or he didn't like lots of people close by.

The next time I called at Bill's home, he took Trim and another young dog to give them both a bit of practice, something I always enjoyed. I held onto Trim so that Bill could work on the other dog, one with a lot of promise. This was its time to be taught to drive the sheep away from the handler. This is the most difficult thing to get any dog to do, as the dog's instinct is to bring animals towards you, not drive away.

I held the young dog while Bill put Trim through his training without a single refusal or mistake. I knew Bill would not have taken this dog to the trial at Lowgill under-trained. I finished up owning Trim, as Bill wasn't willing to take him to another trial to be let down again.

Later on, when Trim had done a lot of work on the fell and amongst a lot of sheep in big rough fields, Bill came to visit. Just as he arrived I had to take a lot of sheep to the fell with Trim, and I was surprised to see his van behind me as I reached the end of the hard road in the High Close. Trim was driving the flock of sheep away from us at that moment. I was about to go with him as far as the gate onto White Bank when Bill said, 'Let the dog take them. Don't give any commands till you have to.'

To our surprise Trim didn't turn round to look where we were until he had gone through the fell gate. Bill said, 'I think he will take those sheep to Slaidburn if you don't call him off!'

34

1947: THE SNOWSTORM, NELL AND MADDIE

The snow had settled into a nearly solid mass and, with the frost each night, it was possible to walk on it without it giving way in midstride when all one's bodyweight was on one leg. Everywhere was glistening white because of the bright sun as I walked up the track towards High Close carrying a ten-foot pole, which I used to prod down into the snow drifts. Sometimes I felt life on the other end, and I had a shovel over my shoulder to dig through the snow to find any sheep that might have survived. My company for the day was Maddie, and Father's dog Nell. Nell came because of her out-standing ability to find life under deep snow.

Nicholas and I had already spent hours each day during the storm digging out living ewes and finding many dead nearby. I searched the hollows in High Close just in case any more could be found. The snow was above the walls by as much as two feet, making it possible to travel from one field to another and not see any part of the boundary fences or walls.

Nell stopped suddenly with her nose close to the snow, on the opposite side of the wall from where she had found ewes the previous day. I pushed the pole to make holes in the snow and Nell stuck her nose into them. She moved from one hole to another and I thought, 'These are all dead.' Then, all at once, she started to dig with her front feet. I knew there would be life. The nearer I dug to the living ewes, the more fuss she made, trying to help and many times making it difficult to dig near her.

I found four live ewes and two dead ones. With a struggle, we managed to move those live ewes into Low Close. They were not able to walk home as they had been held down in their resting positions for at least one week, judging by the weight of the snow that had covered them. All I had to give them was a few handfuls of cattle nuts, which I had taken along just in case.

I searched along the wall side, prodding

with the pole every two or three feet. Nell went ahead, hardly bothering to put her head down to sniff. We tried all the hollows further on, past the area that was wired around with a red notice attached that said, 'Unexploded bombs. Keep out'.

Nell, Maddie and I were well away from the wired area when the snow gave way under me and the shovel fell to one side. The fall seemed to be in slow motion as I was going down what turned out to be a trench bomb crater, about fifteen feet deep and three feet wide, with water to within five feet of ground level.

Luckily I had held on to the pole and somehow turned it to cross the top of the hole. I prayed that the pole would not break and carefully moved each hand as near to the side of the hole as possible, all the time trying to keep calm. The sides of the crater, which I will call a well, as that is the best way to describe it, were slimy with no foothold or handhold, but I was determined not to panic. All I can say is that I used every ounce of my strength to get out of there. I knew that if I did not succeed, my body would never be found and no one would know what had happened.

On top, I lay for a long time. Both dogs

knew that I was exhausted and they were licking me and trying to get as close to me as possible. I tried not to think too deeply about it because, had my pole broken, my chances of survival would have been slim.

The journey home passed without my noticing it, as I was thinking how lucky I was to be alive. I changed into dry clothes, Nicholas fed the dogs and I didn't help with the farm work that evening. A big fire was going in the living room because Mother had been baking. The heat from the fire helped to stop the shivers and, when asked how I had managed to get so dirty and wet, I just said that I had fallen.

On the following day, hay and cattle nuts were taken to the four ewes, which had survived without food for seven days. We were happy to find them alive and able to walk a short distance to better shelter.

35

ANOTHER CLOSE SHAVE

I had spent most of the day in the snow on the fell in the hope that some more sheep could be found alive in the gullies or in the nearest fold. I did find eight sheep which had managed to find rushes still standing through the snow, but decided to leave them where they were. I gave them the cattle feed which I had carried with me in my shoulder bag. I did what I could with my shovel to clear a small area, to make it easier for them to get grass. As soon as they saw it, I had to work hard to keep out of their way.

I now had to make my way home to get there before dark. I got back to the easier going and stopped at the sheep fold near the gateway into High Close. The snow was hard in places and would hold my weight, but often the snow would give way and this made walking very hard work.

I sat down on a through stone in the fold, as I was warm and ready for stopping. Nell and Spy sat as close to me as possible and, with the snow being deep enough, I was on their level. With their warm bodies so near, I dozed off whilst it was still daylight.

Next thing I was aware of, one of the dogs nipped my leg. It had gone very dark. I was stiff and cold but made haste to get home, hoping not to meet someone looking for me.

When I arrived home, Charles and Edgar from Mallowdale were there. They were about to search for me and Charles's first words were, 'Did you sit on a through stone in the first sheep fold, because one of my relatives died on that stone after looking for sheep? Never stop anywhere like that.'

36

ONE-EYE REFUSES

The hard weather conditions of the 1946–47 winter meant that hay time came late that year. The last of the snow did not melt from the hollows on Mallowdale Fell until the middle of June. As a result, the sheep that had survived the winter with their lambs stayed in the meadow into May to help them recover. Haymaking was put off until late in July.

Now I had used One-Eye for most of the farm work I did, as well as using her to take the milk to the milk stand and going to collect the groceries. The day we decided to cut the first setting in the big front meadow, Father wanted to use One-Eye and a bay horse called Tom.

Nicholas helped to take the two-horse mowing machine into the meadow. That day I took the milk using a grey horse called Dapple. She had been off work for twelve months after injuring her near-hind fetlock. She had been brought back to work gently, doing only light jobs, and this was her first time on the road since the injury.

I put the three churns into the milk float, fastening them to the side and wondering how she would cope on the steep hills, especially Barkin. As I drove past Father and Nicholas, the cutter bar was down and they were nearly ready to start cutting the grass. I didn't give them another thought as I was watching Dapple, making sure she did nothing that would hurt her hind leg which had healed so well.

When we arrived at the milk stand there

were three other farmers there, chatting together after putting their churns on the stand.

'Tha's got a fancy horse today. What's up wi' One-Eye?' said one of them.

'Father and Nicholas are cutting grass in the front meadow,' I replied.

'Oh, so tha'll hev to put up wi' this un till after thi' father's dun't hay then. Wheniver I've seen thee a'fore tha's had that one-eyed horse. It's a wonder tha doesn't let her come by hersel',' he said, with a laugh.

'I haven't taught her how to lift the churns onto the stand yet,' I replied, also laughing.

After this bit of banter, I lifted the churns onto the stand and one of the men passed three empty churns for me to take back home. The ring those three empty steel churns made when being put together on the float made Dapple uneasy. Seeing this, Ronnie, one of the men, went to her head to calm her. I tied the rope round the churns as tight as I could, hoping the ringing caused as the float went over bumps wouldn't upset her.

After we had gone about half a mile she settled and then she had to keep her mind on the job, as we were going down Barkin. As we passed Middle Salter barn, we came to the entrance gate to Higher Salter. We went through and I fastened the gate and got back into the float. To my surprise, no grass had been cut and I wondered what had gone wrong, as my task had taken an hour. When I drove Dapple nearer home, I saw Nicholas standing by the wall. Father had the long reins in his hand and his face was red with stress and sweat. I was worried, because he was recovering from an accident, so I said, 'Calm down and take Dapple home. I'll see if I can make a do.'

I knew that, for the first time in his many dealings with horses, he found it hard to accept that these two fully-broken horses had refused to straighten the chains. All the horses had done, up to then, was to trample an area of mowing grass and no grass had been cut.

Nicholas and Father took Dapple home, took the churns into the kitchen to be washed, and then unyoked, fed and groomed her. Meanwhile, I fastened the long reins to the seat of the mower. I went to One-Eye and stroked her nose, talking to her in the hope she would calm down. Gradually her muscles stopped shaking. Still talking to her, I untied the reins, sat on the seat and, hoping the two horses had settled down, said calmly, 'Come on, lass. Go on, Tom.'

Off they went, much to my relief. Now when cutting grass with horses, farmers cut an area of about two acres, called a 'setting', and we did this with no problem. Father and Nicholas arrived back as the last bit of grass was cut. They had been watching me from a distance. Father said 'That one-eyed horse is the first one ever to refuse to work for me, so let's keep back and not upset her.'

In spite of this, she was such a likeable horse that he couldn't help giving her a pat on the neck. We decided that One-Eye had got so used to me, my ways and my voice, that when, for the first time in two years, a new voice told her to 'Walk on', she was having none of it. After that episode, Father would feed her along with the other horses, but never once did he use her in harness.

A lot of water has gone under the bridge since 1947 but I can still picture that really special horse.

37

LEAVING HOME

Father had now made a full recovery from an injury to his back, which had kept him off work for nearly two years. During that time Nicholas and I had done all the farm work for little pay. I had to take over the business, making all the business decisions as well as organising the seasonal work. We had to take over the haymaking, clipping, dipping, lambing, and sheep sales, together with the everyday chores, such as milking the few cows by hand, calf-feeding, and looking after the horses and dogs. We worked together to get the best results possible from all the stock. Through the two lambing seasons we spent very little time in our beds, as we needed to help any ewes having difficulty lambing.

It was now the first week in November 1950. All the sheep sales and wether lamb sales were almost over. The rams, bought in Lanark Auction, had arrived and were in the front meadow, waiting for their seasonal freedom amongst the ewes.

The doctor had said that Father was now fit to work. We were having our midday meal when, with no tact or consideration, Mother said, 'Now your father is better, he is going to run things.' There was no mention of the work we had done to keep the farm going, or of the healthy bank balance that I had managed to achieve.

'If this is the case,' I said, 'Nicholas and I want proper wages each week.'

The reply was, 'You only have to ask when you need any money. All this will be yours when I'm gone.'

My reply was, 'I want a wage for the work I do now. I don't want to sit across the table, hoping and wondering how soon that will be.'

I could tell, by their attitude that getting a wage was out of the question. That same day, Timothy Longton arrived in the yard needing a shepherd. He was the manager at Whitendale now that the Handley family had left the farm. He knew there were three of us and called to see if anyone would work for him. Without any talk of wages, I got my few clothes together, put my dog Maddie on a lead, and we were soon in his Austin Ten car and on our way to Whitendale.

It was more than twenty miles by road, but seven hard miles over the moor. On the journey, Tim wanted to know what had happened as I had not even enquired about wages, conditions of work or even where I was to sleep. When I told him all that had been said at Higher Salter, especially about Mother's attitude, he understood.

This was the first time I lived with a family, outside close relations. The nearer we got to the large farm, the more I wondered what this new life would be like. Tim led the way to the clean kennels, a block of four, all with separate runs. The kennel on the left was to be Maddie's new home. With my few belongings, we went into the house. I was still feeling nervous.

38

WHITENDALE

As result of the heavy snow storms of 1947, hardly any draft ewes were sold that back end. On most farms so many sheep of all ages had lost so much condition even if they lived, and many had dead lambs. Of those sheep that managed to carry lambs through alive, only a few had enough milk to feed one lamb.

When the lambing season started at Whitendale, I cannot remember one dry day. We needed to wear knee leggings, waterproof coats and sou'westers at all times. The ewes' fleeces held so much water, it made the sheep difficult to handle especially when a lamb needed help to feed or, as often happened, a ewe lost her lamb and a foster lamb, taken from twins or from a ewe with no milk, had to be mothered on. I remember thinking at the time, 'Why is there so much rain when the ewes are lambing? It's spring, a time for sunshine and dry spells, not heavy rain every day.' My previous lambing at Higher Salter had been much the same.

Tim and I spent every spare moment in the hut in the croft, which had sheep pens on either side where we had ewes and lambs needing attention. As we worked side by side, we both lost our sense of humour and only said what was necessary. The older ewes from two years before should have gone as draft ewes but had to be kept to make up the numbers to what the fell could carry. These ewes were our problem.

Then the sun started to shine and life got back to normal. Mr Longton, Tim's father, came for an afternoon visit. His company made both of us feel that we hadn't done as bad a job as we thought we had. Believe me, my confidence and love of shepherding was at rock bottom.

Mr Longton had won many sheepdog trials from a very young age and all his sons, and now some of his grandsons and great-grandsons have followed in his footsteps. Tim and his bitch Nell had recently won the International Sheepdog Trials, the most coveted prize. This did not surprise me as I had seen her at work amongst the sheep; she knew what Tim wanted her to do without commands.

We were sitting at the table, having eaten the first course, when dogs crept into the conversation. Nell had won the first of the season's sheepdog trials, even after the hard work she had done during lambing. Mrs Longton and I listened with interest to all that had happened at the trial and who Tim met to speak to. Tim's brother, Tot, came second, in the well-attended trial.

I chose the wrong moment and said, 'I wouldn't swop Maddie for any other dog.'

The Wednesday following, when Tim and

family had been to Bentham on business, they arrived in the yard as I was feeding the dogs. Tim came towards me and handed me a pink form. I read it and realised that it was an entry form for Lowgill Sheepdog Trials. I knew what he was about to say. 'You will see the entry form is made out. I've entered you and Maddie to run at Lowgill. The trial is two weeks come Saturday. Then we'll know how good she is.'

Every night after the evening meal, I went well away from the house to spend time making sure Maddie would do what I wanted. I had another bitch at the time which I used for the heavy work, then Maddie could rest and get used to handling six ewes instead of large numbers.

Soon it was the Saturday of the trial. I stayed up late the night before, but I was so wound up I didn't sleep so well. During the journey in Tim's Land Rover we had very little conversation, and all the time I was regretting my statement made at the table, especially when Tim was in high spirits, having won again with Nell.

My turn came to run Maddie and I was determined not to let her down. The man I had bought her from was a contestant and many other people knew how she was bred.

They had no idea what to expect, as neither Maddie nor I had taken part in a sheepdog trial. Maddie ran better than I expected and took the hogs around the trial course without any hesitation, then penned at the first attempt. My knees were knocking in terror all the time, because many top shepherds and trial men were now standing behind the roped-off area.

Maddie was now in the back of the Land Rover, and I went to watch the trial continue, feeling thankful that I hadn't made a fool of myself. To my surprise, I was congratulated many times by men I admired for their skills. Best of all, Harry Huddleston gave me a slap on my back that nearly knocked me over, and said, 'I'll give you twice what you paid me for Maddie. No one will have a better run than she did.'

Back at Whitendale, Mrs Longton was eager to know how we had done but neither of us said anything. We had the drink she had ready for us and then went out to finish our evening chores. Halfway through the evening meal, when there had been no mention of the day at Lowgill Sheepdog Trials, Mrs Longton said, 'Well, am I not to know how well or badly either of you have done?'

I waited for Tim to speak, as there was no

way I would have told her that I won, but Tim told her. She slapped me on the shoulder and said, 'Well done, Bill!'

Working a dog at a trial in front of lots of experienced handlers is not easy.

39

GETTING READY TO LEAVE HIGHER SALTER

I had returned home after the last lamb was born at Whitendale. In the spring of 1950, we persuaded Father to get permission to look over a lowland farm, Layhead Farm, near Rathmell. A letter arrived giving a date, a time and permission to look round the house and the land with the agent.

Nicholas and I were busy walling between High Close and Gudber Fell, as we had to get the walls in good order that were connected with our rented land. Our chat, as we worked, was about our hopes that Father would like the place they had gone to look at, and he could come to some agreement with the agent about the rent.

We went on about our reasons for leaving Higher Salter. The place was too big for Father to manage by himself even with the help of a hired man, if it were possible to find anyone to live in so far away from the nearest village and even further from Lancaster. Nicholas had had his eighteenth birthday not long before and I was in my twenty-first year. We wanted to make our own way, earning a proper wage, not pocket money like now. My advice to anyone is don't work for parents, as they would rather pay hired help the money they were due than give pocket money to their sons.

Father and Mother arrived home as evening work was nearly finished and soon we were sitting at the table, eating our meal without mentioning Layhead or their journey. A few days later, Father wanted to know how many gaps were still to be put up in High Close. About five or six, we told him. He went on to say that we needed to press on and get them finished so he could give notice to our landlord that we would be leaving on May 12th the following spring.

We must have looked surprised, because he went on to tell us that he had taken the tenancy of Layhead Farm. This made all the difference to us, as we could now see our way forward.

That summer and back end seemed to pass quickly, because we had so much to get through and wanted to leave the place in better order than when we took it over. We spent the next three weeks putting up the last of the wall gaps between High Close and Gudber Fell and, as we worked, we talked about all the jobs ahead – shearing, haymaking, lamb sales, draft ewe sales, and getting the farm to look as though someone lived and worked there.

The one thing neither of us was happy about was that this would be our last year shepherding on the fell or in fields as large as these, with different dogs, some very good and others not so good. Owning a good dog amongst a lot of sheep and working them over a large area was a part of my life that even now gives me pleasure as I write about it. Dogs that we broke in to whistles and others, with different natures, to which we taught voice commands, have come up in conversations many times over the years with my brother and other people.

During the months that followed we were kept busy with seasonal work, gathering, shearing and haymaking. We also helped our neighbours at Mallowdale to gather their sheep, and spent the next few days there, clipping, castrating and marking, so the bulk of them could go back to the fell.

Friendships can be tested when many men are working together amongst big numbers of ewes and lambs. There will always be one dog that finds it easy to be in the wrong place at a most crucial moment, making more work for the other tired and willing dogs. When the last of the sheep and lambs were back on the fell, clipped, dosed and dipped, the ones that did not pass the fitness test or had broken mouths were kept on better grazing, to be sold later. Thankfully, there were not many of these.

Haymaking started without much of a break. Father cut the grass from the track that led to Mallowdale to the croft wall, using One-Eye and Tom, the only horses we had at the time. Nicholas and I spent all day checking the ewes and lambs, finding most of them on their own patch on the fell. They always knew where to go. Father was good at forecasting the weather and he could tell, even though the day was dull and drizzly, when we were in for a dry spell.

To our surprise, he asked a contractor with a grey Ferguson tractor with a mounted mower to come and cut the rest of the big meadow. The only other tractor ever to have worked on Higher Salter was when the War Agg ploughed part of big meadow to reseed it. We were amazed how quickly this work was done. He only stopped to replace the blunt cutting blade with a sharpened one and to have his meals. It was easy to see that the days of the work horse were numbered, because the tractor never got tired.

With a good crop of the best hay we had ever managed to get in the barns, and the bays full to the main beams, Father began wondering if he had done right to give up the tenancy. After such a hard time of nonstop work, the everyday jobs were like a rest period.

The store lambs sales were soon upon us and we had to gather the ewes and their lambs for weaning. We could hear the sound of bleating lambs wanting to get back to their mothers. Some mothers could jump over the high walls and would be found back in the meadow with their offspring. Sorting lambs into lots of twenty and marking each lot on a different part, from the forehead to the rump, then starting again with a second colour for the lambs in the next set, took time.

The lambs were entered at Lancaster

Auction Mart for a special sale, the Littledale and Roeburndale Lamb Sale, held in October. The lambs had to walk two miles to the gateway below Thorn Bush Farm, as that was the best place for loading. The hills were too steep from Higher Salter for them to travel safely when there were two decks full inside the lorry and also lambs on the top deck. Loading was achieved, however, and by that time everyone, including the dogs, was shattered and that was only the start of the day.

At the Auction Mart no time was wasted sorting the lambs into pens of twenty. Lorries were waiting to unload quickly so they could pick up another load. This was one of the best sales of the year and it was well-attended. Here lowland farmers could buy store lambs from the hill farms and many returned each year to buy lambs from the same fell farms, especially when the lambs bought before had been fattened and made good money for them.

Higher Salter lambs always sold well and this was our main source of income. A ballot was drawn at the beginning of most sales to give each lot a fair chance. Those that were drawn to be sold first, before buyers had settled to what prices they were prepared to pay, were often at a disadvantage.

The same applied at the end of the day, when there were large numbers of stock to be sold. Often it would be after dark when the last lot came into the ring and this would be a worry, as most of the buyers were lowland farmers with many dairy cows and followers which needed attention. The farmers selling hoped the customers would still be there and that the higher prices, achieved earlier, would be maintained.

Higher Salter lambs were sold at about three o'clock in the afternoon and made the top price of the day. We had hoped earlier in the day that we would have a good sale, as a lot of buyers had looked them over more than once and made favourable remarks. We returned home feeling good for once, knowing our year's labours would put the bank balance well into the black.

40

LAYHEAD

All the grazing was rented out at Mr Harrisons's retirement sale to farmers in the area, and made more than Father was willing to pay for grazing sheep. We had the grazing at Higher Salter until the February 14th, 1951. It was then that Father rented two fields very near to Giggleswick for the forty gimmer hogs that were over the number that Mr G. Ibbottson wanted when he took over.

The hogs were taken by lorry just after the 14th and would have to be seen every day, to make sure the change from moorland onto rich grazing didn't harm them. One week later I drove One-Eye, yoked in a cart loaded with tools and some feed for her, along with a change of clothes, boots and wellingtons, as I had to stay at Layhead and live with the Harrisons to do the spring work there.

It was a bright sunny spring day and One-Eye covered the eighteen or so miles, only stopping for feed and water. Our first stop was at Green Smithy to have her shoes checked, to make sure all four were secure for the rest of the journey. Mr Taylor, the blacksmith, told me to let her walk at her own pace and stop for a rest after five or six miles, and this I did. One-Eye could out-walk any other horse and the cart had rubber tyres and an easy load. She could manage and not even sweat. I enjoyed the experience, seeing the countryside at walking pace, sitting on a bale of hay in the cart, high enough to look over the hedges and walls, with the only sound coming from One-Eye's hooves on the hard road.

My brother came by car most days to look at the hogs at Giggleswick and bring food for our midday meal and a snack for mid-afternoon. Every day we were busy carting muck into heaps, seven yards apart, on the meadows we were to take over. We gave One-Eye a rest for a day as we spread the heaps set out the day before with the forks we used for loading. The mechanical spreader was only seen on large farms.

On Saturday afternoon, we went home to Higher Salter and returned on Monday, because Mr Harrison agreed to feed and water One-Eye. I must say that when we started, the middens were full to overflowing and the heap in the croft looked no less at the end of our first day's work. Comments were made in the village about the hours we worked and the amount of muck we carted each day.

On the 12th of May, the Harrisons moved out and the Newby family took possession. All the spring work was well in hand and the grass in the meadows was better than any we were used to. At the table, having eaten our first meal together at this new farm in the lowlands of the Ribble valley, Father was asked, 'Are you happy with the place and will you settle to this way of life?'

All he would say was, 'The fields are smaller and it's a lot warmer, but there's not much work for a good dog.'

He, like us, would miss all that.

41

CLIFTON HALL FARMS

On the 4th of June 1959, I started work, as shepherd at Clifton Hall Farms, about four miles from Preston, in the Fylde Valley. My new home was a lovely two-bedroomed cottage with a bathroom. Downstairs there was a lounge, a kitchen large enough for a dining table and chairs and a scullery on the left of the door. Outside was a long back garden.

Opposite the back door was a shed made of corrugated iron, which was about ten feet square, and past that was the water toilet. At the bottom of the garden there was the coal shed, with brick walls and tiled roof. Gem's kennel stood on the concrete area between the toilet and the coal shed. Having a well-bred working dog again was like old times.

Most of the land consisted of big flat fields that surrounded the village of Clifton and reached down to the River Ribble, and there was a large area of marshland which flooded when the spring tides were followed by high winds. As well as looking after the sheep every day, I checked the cattle when they were outside grazing to see them and to keep a lookout for any injuries or illness. The sheep were mules, a cross between horned ewes and Leicestershire rams, kept for breeding fat lambs. They were much larger than the fell ewes that I had been accustomed to.

Haymaking was in full swing, with hundreds of bales ready for carting in to the large barns on long four-wheeled trailers with an axle at each end, where the front axle would pivot each way. The tractor men could reverse a loaded trailer into the barn and put it exactly where it had to be to offload. It was some time before I had the confidence to put a loaded trailer into a tight area!

My work started each day at seven a.m. when I went with my dog Gem to see the stock on different parts of the farm, to move any that needed a change onto fresh grazing, to bring back to the farm any fat stock to be sold in Preston Auction and then hopefully to have time to go back to my cottage for some breakfast.

Keeping the yards clean and tidy was very important. Whenever cattle or sheep had been in the pens, even for a short time, the place had to be left spotless.

After lunch, eight men were sent with three tractors and trailers down into the fields to load two and leave one to be loaded by three men, me being one of them. My job from then on was to be on each trailer loading, with Norman and Peter throwing the bales up to me. When a trailer was unloaded in one of the barns, it would be brought back to the field and the one we had loaded was taken back to the barn. The weather was hot and sunny that summer, which meant nonstop work until dark each day. I was glad as I needed the overtime money.

Harvest followed with hardly any break. Norman, the cowman, and I spent all our spare time loading bags of grain from the ground onto trailers. Most of the bags weighed above one and a half hundredweights each when the crop was barley or oats. When the wheat was combined, the bags looked smaller, yet many exceeded two hundredweights. The men offloading in the grain store complained and blamed Norman and me. We were never near enough to the combine to say anything and, even if we had, they would not have listened.

The bags were filled on the combine and the chap bagging off often made the bags heavy on purpose. Ted Smith, the manager, got wind of this. The next day, with two trailers still loaded with the bags the man had filled standing in the grain store from the day before, the bagger was given the job of unloading the heavy bags he had filled to teach him a lesson. He was replaced by another chap on the combine. Ted Smith was a good boss and he didn't miss a trick. The work on the ploughed fields never stopped, what with potatoes, turnips and kale to be carted off.

Most of my time was spent amongst the sheep, dipping, sorting lots for different rams that had to be raddled each day. Lame sheep were a problem, as their feet were hardly ever free of soil or muck because of the lush flat ground

On December 28th 1969, I married Edna Graham at the Congregational Church in Kirkham and our wedding reception was at the Swan Hotel. I had enough holiday owing for us to spend our week's honeymoon in Southport. Edna was a teacher, a job she enjoyed, and she started at a new school in Blackpool.

Lambing began about February 15th. The ewes had plenty of milk and most of them had twins. The ones that had three lambs needed special attention and they had to be taken inside each night into separate pens; left outside, lambs would wander off and, even with numbers marked on each set, too much time was lost keeping them together. With the ewes that had just one lamb, I took the smallest one off a set of three of the same age and hoped the mothering on would be successful and the lamb would have a better chance.

All the workmen at the time got on with one another very well. Most of them had family and many of the sixteen had worked on the estate for a number of years. As long as each member of staff pulled his weight, the manager was happy.

Lorries came every working day to take away potatoes as they were harvested and sorted. Most of the grain went away too and the fat cattle numbers varied each week, depending on how many were ready for the butcher. The lambs were the same, with only ten or twenty some weeks. On one particular week there were one hundred lambs ready and this pleased the manager, as lamb trade that week was good. This made my job easier as there were fewer animals needing attention.

That summer I was due two weeks off

work and Edna arranged for the two of us to spend most of our holiday in Switzerland. This really put me on my mettle, as I had never been abroad before nor had I driven a car on the right or driven onto a ferry. That holiday was the best ever, as it had never entered my head to drive so far, to stay in a hotel in Paris and then drive on to a beautiful village near Zurich called Lachen. The hotel was so lush and the staff so friendly.

Back at work the chaps wanted to know what we had done and everything about the holiday. I tried not to make too much of it, as none of them were able to go abroad at the time; most of them had families and none of their wives went to work.

Everything went well on the farm for quite a spell and then things changed for the worse for all of us who worked there. Mr Smith's son, Tom, was badly hurt through riding on the drawbar of the tractor. His mate was driving the tractor which was pulling a muck spreader. Tom's foot slipped, the power shaft grabbed his clothes and, in a flash, pulled him between the power shaft and the drawbar, causing severe injuries. Tom was in hospital for months. We were in shock. When Tom came out of hospital at last, still not fit to come back to work, Mr Smith gave his notice to leave his post as manager. I, for one, was unhappy to see him go.

Rumours as to who would be the next manager were rife and there were lots of discussions and guesses about who would get the job. To everyone's dismay, the 'odd-job man' became our boss. I lost my job as shepherd to his oldest son, who couldn't work a sheepdog. My new job was as a dairyman and I was given no choice, as anyone who grumbled in any way was told he could leave, even though his home was a tied cottage and his children were at a school in the area.

Not one of us understood why Mr Pickles gave the job of manager to a man with no experience and no idea how to handle staff. Within six months, twelve of the men, together with their families, had been replaced by men of his choice. Like him, they had very little experience.

The dairy cows were pedigree Ayrshires. I didn't worry too much, as I had managed a pedigree herd before. At the time, farm workers' wages increased a 'staggering' seven shillings a week! Norman and I would take turns each night, when the cows were inside for winter, to check that all was well. We were paid extra for the half an hour's work to do this and that was all we got, even if one or more cows happened to calve after hours.

The rise in wages made the manager take over the job of checking the cows at nights and weekends. Needless to say, on the very first morning after he took over, Norman and I opened the door into the big shippon to find some cows standing crossways in their stalls. There was dung in many feed troughs and water bowls, fifteen newborn calves sliding in the dung behind and underneath cows, not their mothers, and cows that had calved bawling for their calves. I could go on and on and still not paint the picture as bad as it was.

All the calves were pushed or dragged into the fodder gang in front of the cows, and then we cleaned out the troughs and water bowls before any concentrates could be fed. By the time all this was done, we were one-and-a-half hours behind and the milk lorry was waiting at the milk stand.

The manager now lived in Clifton House, close to the milk stand. He could see the milk lorry waiting; we knew what was about to happen and it did. He came blustering into the shippon as we were milking the last eight cows, didn't ask what had gone wrong, just started shouting and cursing, with the F word used every other word. He could not even see the obvious signs as to why we were late, even though the shippon was in such an untidy state. Norman and I ignored him, doing our best to get the milk off the cooler and loaded onto the waiting lorry.

Even with our filthy milking coats, which we removed in front of him, he still had no idea that something must have gone wrong. We turned to go for our breakfast; by this time it was ten o'clock and we were weak with hunger.

The manager was fuming, and he shouted, 'Where the hell do you think you're going?'

I could see Norman was not going to say anything and by now my hackles were up. I went towards him to say, 'Don't ever swear at me again when I'm doing my job. No one checked the cows last night. The proof is in the fodder gangway!'

I left him dumbstruck and went to get my breakfast. On our return from breakfast, we found him and his two sons trying to figure out how to put each calf, being pedigree, with its dam. It was impossible and this meant the six heifer calves, kept for breeding, could not be registered. We often wondered how he kept his job, or who got the blame.

The friendly atmosphere of the whole Clifton Hall Estate changed, as nobody who worked there felt secure. Edna and I began to look in the papers, hoping to find an alternative to farming, but kept this to ourselves.

After looking at many options, we bought a shop selling groceries and lots of ice cream, called Sunnyside, on the edge of Great Harwood. All was in place for us to take over the shop, so the time came to hand in my notice. It was pay day and the manager drove round in his car to give each man his wages, as they were on different parts of the estate doing their work. I wondered what to expect when I handed in my notice. As dairymen were hard to find, and the reputation of some farmers was well known, if staff were always changing, applicants were wary. I can say that he wasn't pleased, as he liked to be the one to tell a man he had lost his job.

Two weeks later, Edna and I moved out of our lovely cottage. The removal man and I had to take out the bedroom window to get our bed out of the house, as the stairs were too narrow. That was the end of farming for me for many years. As for my dog, Gem, the manager had already taken her out of her kennel at the back of the cottage when Edna was at work, teaching in Blackpool, and I was at work on the farm on my first day as a dairyman. We were both upset, as it was done without telling me. Edna never forgave him, as it was stealing, and would not speak to him when he tried to say goodbye to her when we left.

When Mr Smith was the manager, he had lent me the money to buy Gem and I had agreed for him to take a pound a week off my wages, which he did. This new manager said there was no reference to this agreement in the books and there was not a thing I could do to prove she was mine. Gem was keen to work and to be among sheep was all she lived for. They worked her till her feet were so sore she couldn't walk. Later on I asked Jack Tye about Gem and was told she had died shortly after we had moved away.

It wasn't long before all the animals were sold at Clifton, followed by a big machinery sale, and all the land was let off. The now ex-manager was offered the tenancy of the smallest farm on the estate, near the river, and he went there with his family.

Years later I met the man who followed them when they left that small farm and he told me the place was a disgrace. The long wooden sheds had to be pulled down before they could shift the dung that was so deep inside the doorways. This had to be cleared to get the bullocks out in order to be sold at the ex-manager's sale.

42

EDGEBANK FARM

We had an offer for Sunnyside, which we accepted. Through Mr Nickson, we bought Lower Green Post Office at Poulton-Le-Fylde. Edna ran the Post Office and I ran the newspaper, sweets, tobacco and toys' side. We employed two girls to work for us. Our three children were born during the nine years at the shop.

In 1973 Kenneth Cox, a long-time friend, and I attended an Auction Sale at the Town Hall in Kendal. The farm for sale was Edge-bank Farm, Skelsmergh. Edna stayed at our house, on Larch Grove, which we had bought when we moved from Poulton, looking after the children. Mr Gillies, the ex-tenant of the farm, called to tell Edna that she was now a farmer's wife and the joint owner of Edgebank Farm.

We put our house up for sale as we were to take over the farm in November, which gave us four months before completion. Then we had the oil crisis and house sales came to a standstill. It was the following June before the house sale went through and we finally moved in. In the meantime, Edna had gone back to her profession as a history teacher at Longlands Boys School in Kendal. I took a job with Battle, Hayward and Bower, owners of Felldales, to sell farm supplies in the region.

When I had taken over the farm, I bought in sixty horned ewes, two Teeswater rams and a sheepdog called Jet. I organised the major repairs to the farmhouse whilst we were still living in Kendal, and proceeded to farm from a distance of two miles. That first spring of 1974 my sheep had their lambs, and a retired farmer from Kendal went to look at the lambing ewes at midday. Many times after work Edna and the children went up in the car to make sure all was well.

The farmhouse was a typical Lakeland house, with four front-facing windows and a porch between the two bottom ones. The children thought it looked like a house a child would draw. The view from the house and anywhere on the farm is of Kendal Castle, on a hill above the town, and the green fields of the many farms in the valley. To the west and north are the Cumbrian Hills.

During our stay there, the livestock increased. Robert (our son) took on the job of feeding the hens and putting them inside at night, and never once did he forget. When they stopped laying in cold weather and there were no eggs for any length of time, Robert and I would pick a hen which he chose, knowing it to be a poor layer, and get it ready for the oven. A few days later, if Robert collected two eggs, he would say, 'Those hens must be scared Dad! They must know the next time they miss laying an egg, we'll have another one of them for dinner!'

We always kept the hen food in a milk churn in the feed store. There were times when the lid was not replaced. One day Robert went to the house to tell his mum that he needed 'Mother Cat' as there was a mouse in the churn, eating the food. He picked up the cat in his arms and ran to the feed store. The cat leapt out of his arms, headfirst into the churn, got the mouse in her mouth and jumped out before he had time to move back. Edna was busy making the meal, and wondered what had happened when Robert came through the door. He said, 'Mum you should have seen how quickly Mother Cat got that mouse. She gave me a fright!' He was seven years old at the time.

Our family, now adults, often mention their happy times at Edgebank Farm, with freedom to play outside, but always with the warning never to go near the tarn we had on our land. They now tell us they climbed the tree above the water trough to a height which would have terrified us, had we known.

One time Robert and Andrew, a friend from a farm close by, were playing in the barn because the weather was not suitable for playing outside. Edna and I thought they would be safe in there with plenty of room to play ball games. When lunch was ready I went to tell them, to find Andrew on the highest crossbar of the A-frame, swinging his legs with no thought of the height or the distance from the barn floor. The only thing I could think of at the time was to say, 'Come on lads. It's food time.' I moved out of sight, praying he would get down on his own. If I had stayed, he may have lost his nerve. What a relief when they came through the barn door as if nothing had happened. All I could think was, what I would have said to his parents, had he fallen from that height onto the stone floor?

In early June 1975, a few weeks before Sally's eleventh birthday, I called at a farm in the Lythe Valley, as a sales rep. for B.H. and B., to find the farmer busy getting some Welsh Mountain ponies into a big pen. I left the van well away and went to help turning them in, as they were trying to break away near to me. With a bit of calm handling the ponies went through the gate and settled down. The farmer knew the company I worked for, but the only thing on his mind were the ponies. He thanked me for helping, knowing if I hadn't been there just then the ponies would not be in the pen. I asked if they were for sale.

'Why?' he said. 'Do you want to buy one?'

With a bit of bartering, I bought two which I had taken a fancy to as I looked over the gate. I paid for them there and then, on condition he arranged for their carriage home.

Sally was in the house, helping Mum, when Mr Nelson turned his lorry around in the yard to unload in the gateway. The ponies had travelled loose as they were un-broken. Sally was asked to come out to help, with no idea what had arrived. The ramp doors were let down and every one moved out of the way as two dark grey ponies came down the lorry ramp to stand in the yard. Sally's birthday present could not have been any better.

Her pony was registered as 'Lythe Jasmine' and, with a bit of help from me, Sally spent all her spare time mouthing her, then driving her with long reins, until it was time to get on her back. All went well, even when the saddle was on and the girth pulled tight. It wasn't long before Jane, at the age of five, was able to ride with Sally leading Jasmine. Soon Jane didn't need help and became a competent little rider. Sally and Jane spent many happy hours in the meadow. Robert had no interest in horses!

As for the other pony, Lythe Gaye, hers is another interesting story.

Gaye was only halter broken, as all our spare time had been spent on making sure Jasmine was good to handle. It was decided that as she was such a good type and very well-bred, we would put her to a very well-bred Welsh Mountain stallion belonging to one of our neighbours. We would let her have one foal and then break her for riding. Her filly foal was born during the night and she was already standing and suckling when I went into the field to check. I wondered how soon it would be before all the family were in the field, looking at that baby pony. I cannot describe their pleasure as they crossed the meadow to find the foal frisking about on long thin legs. It was the first of June 1975.

The foal's registered name was Edgebank Amber and, during the next twelve months, it was easy to see that she was a very good type. The owner of the stallion called to look her over, taking his time, a very good sign. Although he said very little, I knew he was pleased with his stallion's progeny. Before he went, he wanted to know what I intended doing with the foal, as he would be interested in buying her in a few months' time.

He called again a few weeks later, asking me to put a price on her. I had given thought to this from time to time, as she was developing well. I had told the family that Amber would be sold to our neighbour because he took his best ponies to shows. The first show he took her to she won!

Our two daughters were both good riders now, as they spent many hours each week with the ponies. With Sally having outgrown Jasmine, we decided to sell Gaye at Wigton horse sale. We spent time getting her into top condition, both in appearance and handling, to give her every chance to make her worth.

Sally came along to the sale and enjoyed the experience. As we led Gaye from the trailer to the pen to have her entrance ticket glued on her hip, there were comments from bystanders and a lot of interest. At first Sally rode her bareback up and down with me holding the lead rein, but she soon settled down. Even though Gaye was lively and quick moving, Sally could handle her.

Our time came to take her into the sale ring, followed in by many of the men who had looked her over outside. When the last bid was taken in such a short time, I wondered if I had heard the last bid correctly, and before the auctioneer brought down his gavel I asked him to repeat it. I was satisfied; she was sold to a man who was buying her for a lady in Scotland. A few days later I had a telephone call from her, asking for Gaye's pedigree papers to be sent to her address. The last we saw of Gaye was when we were watching The Horse of the Year Show on TV, where she was in the young riders' competition. How good to know Gaye was doing so well.

To be able to buy a horse of the type and

quality Sally would be proud of and yet at a sensible price, meant buying an unbroken one and starting again from scratch. A few weeks later, I called at The Howe Farm, Troutbeck. Roger Westmorland, as always, invited me into the house for a drink and a bite to eat. Horses came up in conversation, as he had a horse too many. The horse for sale was a two year old, out of a thorough-bred mare by The Shah, a full-bred Arab stallion from the well-known Arab stud close by.

Thinking there was not a hope of buying him, I changed the subject to sheepdogs and then for my reason for calling: to sell him some vaccines and marking for his sheep flock. When I was leaving, Roger wanted me to look at Oliver, as often happened when animals were for sale. It was then that I told him Sally was not interested in going to horse shows or events, and the money avail-able was not enough for me to even think of making an offer.

When I called two days later to deliver the ordered items I found that Mrs Fell, Oliver's owner, had left a message for me to go to the large house across the paddock. To my surprise, as I sat drinking a cup of coffee with her on the opposite side of the table from me, she asked me about Sally. Was she any good at handling horses, would Oliver have a good home with big enough fields to keep him in good condition, and a stable for winter? I told her that the money I could afford was nowhere near the price Oliver would make at auction.

Mrs Fell needed to know if I could break him in to be safe and reliable to ride. Would I be kind to him and not sell him on as soon as he was trained? This was how Oliver became Sally's horse for the next nine years, until she left home to work in London. He was sold on to a good home from whence he was taken to shows and events, where he was very successful.

43

THE SALESMAN

As I have said, I travelled as a salesman to earn extra money when we were settling down at Edgebank. I met many farmers at this time and many unexpected things could happen at any time. I could leave home with a plan for the day, never knowing what the day had in store.

I made calls three times each year before lambing, before shearing and before tupping. I also went to sheep sales, more often than not to collect a debt from a farmer who managed to be out on the day I called at his farm. I understood when this happened because farming income can be difficult. It is the only business where animals go to market with no guarantee as to the money they will make.

One Tuesday there were very few cattle and sheep for sale at Broughton in Furness Auction. My farm calls for the day were from Ravenglass on to Sellafield. I had made three calls, fitting each farmer up with items from my van, which were paid for, and had also collected all the money owing. My next call was past Sellafield to a farm where I only called twice a year, as the lady bought items from my van when she went to Broughton on annual sales' days.

I parked the van, walked to the farmhouse door and was just about to knock, when the lady called, 'Come in, Felldales.' I walked in and there, to my surprise, lying on its side on a pegged rug in front of the fire, was an in-pig young gilt, grunting every time it breathed out and at intervals giving a loud grunt, as though it were dreaming. When I asked about the pig being in the house and how house-trained she was, I was told that Priscilla had been one of a large litter and her dam hadn't enough teats for all of them. Priscilla, from being fed many times each day and night, along with some training, always went to relieve herself across the yard close to the sty where she was born. She was, each day from birth, taken back to her fast-growing family as there was no way Priscilla could have been left alone in the house. With all the attention and time spent with her and having such a good life, they kept putting off stopping her coming into the house through the day.

I asked, 'What will happen when Priscilla gets near to farrowing?'

'Then she will have to stay with her young, but she will always be a pet!' the woman replied.

At this stage I must explain that the room was very clean and tidy, with a blue slate floor, a table and chairs and a television set. As I ate a scone, with tea, and watched Priscilla, a brown Rhode Island Red hen came through the door heading for the television. 'COR, COR, COR,' she said, as she flew onto the telly. As soon as the hen settled,

218

the lady quietly walked across and put her hand behind it. I thought she was going to pick up the hen to take her outside but no: in her hand was a freshly-laid brown egg, caught before it could roll off the sloping back of the telly. The hen stood up, to let everyone know how marvellous she was, saying, 'TOCK-AEK, TOCK-AEK,' and on and on. She then hopped off the telly and walked proudly out of the door.

Once each year, I had to call on farms in Lancashire near Bacup, Todmorden and Littleborough. Our firm had a good name for their products in that area. Most of the calls were to farms well away from tarmac roads. They were mostly stocked with Lonk sheep, tall animals with short thick coats, that did well on the rough land. One farm on my list was along a track that had only ever been used by horse-drawn vehicles. When I arrived in the farmyard in the van, the farmer said, 'That's the first motor to get into this yard from the road.'

I told him why I hadn't met him at the main road the previous day and that there was no way I would let him down. Later he followed me some of the way back along the track, to help me if I had trouble. They must have led a quiet existence!

Visiting farms in outlying areas reminded me of my shepherding days, as most of these farms had flag floors and the cooking fire range with two ovens, one smaller than the other, on the left of the grate, and a water boiler on the right. Some had a crane above the fire, with the two-gallon kettle hanging in place to keep the water in it just short of boiling, for use when needed.

One call in the Todmorden area was to a farm off Todmorden Road. The road to it was steep, with some of the road flagged and some big stone paving, which was very uneven. I parked in the yard near the stable and, to my surprise, I saw two horses in the stable, one in each stall. Seeing them took me back to the days I had enjoyed so much.

One of the farmers came across to me and his first words were, 'Tha must be that Felldales fella fra Kendal.'

'Yes,' I replied.

'Cu thi sen up too't house. Our lad wants to see thi.'

He was a thickset, grey-haired man, with hands that had done a lifetime's hard work, lots of dry stone walling. I followed him into the house and was invited into a place with the flag floors and big cast-iron range, with a drying rack above it. 'Our lad' was much older than the brother I met in the yard and he had the same broad dialect. I was told to sit at the table and to get that pot of tea and beef sandwich into me. When I was near finishing the food, 'Our lad' had his boots off and his feet on a three-legged milking stool. I wondered what was coming.

'Has tu owt on thi van that'll cut these toenails?' he asked.

I looked at his feet to see that his nails were curled round the ends of each toe.

He said, 'I've tried everything. We've nowt that can even cut the little toe. Tha' must have summat. I haven't had mi boots on for days.'

I went to my van. All I could think of were a pair of sheep foot-paring shears, which I always carried. They were made of steel, with straight handles and good V-shaped blades. 'If the shears won't cut his nails, I can't help,' I thought to myself.

I went back into the house and he said, 'Aye them should do. Nay come on, git on with it, I'll shout if tha's hurting mi.'

Well, I never thought anything like this could happen and did I sweat, kneeling in front of a big fire, cutting toenails as thick as these. I was relieved when the job was done with no mishaps. He put his socks on, then his clogs, and did a clog dance round the room.

He paid for the shears and all the other products from the van and, as I drove down the track, I could see them through my side mirror, waving to me. I waved back and pressed my horn. Another satisfied customer!

This Large Print Book, for people
who cannot read normal print,
is published under the auspices of

THE ULVERSCROFT FOUNDATION